40 DAY
Devotional
Challenge
Plus 1

"Do not merely listen to the word...DO what it says!"
James 1:22

by Blair T. Blakeslee

This is a great devotional f...
It can be used with individuals, S... ...ups

D0887085

Endorsements

"Blair Blakeslee is the real deal! He is one of the few guys I've met that truly walks what he talks. He loves Christ and lives a life that is clearly evident of that love. I'm proud to call him a friend. When I read this devotional book, I realized why Blair's life is so reflective of the Jesus he loves. Blair strategically spends time with his God every day and in a way that allows Christ to shape his life. What's more, as someone who practices the presence of God in his own life, Blair can show you how to do the same in your life. Read this book, apply it, and watch your life grow closer to God."

> *Kent Julian: Former Christian & Missionary Alliance National Youth Director, nationally known speaker, author, founder and director of Live It Forward and Speak It Forward. Kent coaches and helps speakers become the best that they can be.*

"This devotional book rocks! Whether you're new at devotions or you've been spending time with God for years, this book will give you a fresh perspective. If you take each day seriously, you will be propelled in your relationship with your Creator and you will begin to crave the time that you spend with Him daily. Throughout our friendship, Pastor Blair Blakeslee has challenged me in my walk with Christ, and I pray that you will use this devotional as you meet Him in the same powerful way."

> *Karen Bishop: Youth pastor at Greenville Alliance Church, vice-president and cofounder of His Work His Way (Greenville)*

"Blair Blakeslee writes this book from years of experience with youth ministry, hours of study of the Scripture and a heart to change a generation. You will be challenged and changed through this 40-day devotional!"

Nichole Schreiber: Pastor and coleader of Chi Alpha College Ministry in northwestern Pennsylvania

Thank You

First, I would like to thank my Lord and Savior Jesus Christ for His love for me. I have felt so inadequate in ministry, but He continues to use me in building His kingdom. I believe with all my heart that He has led me to write this book. I love Him and give Him all the glory and praise.

Second, I thank my wife, Karin, who believed in me and was supportive from start to finish.

Third, I want to thank Bob Lindsey for proofreading half of this book while battling cancer at the same time. He has been a fighter and has not given up letting God use him. He has kept the faith. Thanks, Bob, for devoting and sacrificing your time. I needed someone to make the many, many grammatical corrections. Your work and commitment is appreciated.

Fourth, I would like to thank Nichole Schreiber who also assisted in proofreading this book. Nichole and her husband, Joel, have been great friends of our whole family for a long time. I have enjoyed doing ministry with them over the last many years. Thank you, Nichole, for helping with the proofreading. It has been a huge blessing.

Last but not least, thanks to all those who God has used to inspire, challenge and change my life. It would be impossible to mention all the names, for they include many youth and adults alike. God has blessed me abundantly with an *awesome* church family.

Table of Contents

Testimonial Challenge

Important

Read this before starting your 40-day plus 1 challenge.

For years I have searched for a devotional book that would challenge us to put our faith into practice. I have read different ones. Many were very challenging, but none gave practical ideas on how to put what we read into action.

Four years ago I came across a devotional book called *40-Day Revolution* by Richard Mull. I admired the book because it gives 40 challenges that relate to the daily topic. I, along with many members of our youth group, used the book every fall for three years. During the fourth fall season, some of the youth did not want to go through the same book. Though it was a challenging devotional that I would recommend reading, several teens felt they wanted a devotional with Scripture verses to read followed by a commentary or stories that would help give meaning to the verses. This devotional book does just that, along with giving challenges.

During my days at Houghton College in Houghton, New York, I remember being drawn to a certain passage in the Bible which has greatly influenced my life. Matthew 25:31–46 describes the day when the Lord Jesus judges all the people of all nations. These powerful verses stress the importance of putting our faith into practice and even give specific examples. *If we put our faith into practice like the Word of God commands us to, then lives around us are going to change, including our own!* Let me say this again! *If we put our faith into practice like the Word of God commands us to, then lives around us are going to change, including our own!*

In college, as I read the Gospel accounts, I admired how Jesus was people focused. He was busy doing God's work; and in doing God's work, He was actively touching people's lives. We too are to be busy doing God's work, and that means we must be touching people's lives.

The purpose for this book is to challenge us to carry out the two greatest commandments, found in Matthew 22:37–39: love God with all our total beings and love others like Jesus did. It seems that as Christians we are either "too busy" with our own lives or "too self-focused." As a result, we are not impacting lives around us like God wants us to. I pray that as you read these 40 challenges plus 1, you will allow the Holy Spirit to work in your life and through your life. As you do, amazing things will happen as a testimony of God's greatness!

In James 1:22 it says, *"Do not merely listen to the word, and so deceive yourselves. Do what it says."* As you begin these 40 challenges, you will find yourself "doing" a lot of exciting things. They take time, but if you are persistent, you will be amazed at the testimonies you will have to share because people will be different, including yourself.

The challenges are broken up into different sections.

Days 1–6: These challenges help you to be grounded with the Lord, both through your quiet time with God and by self-examining your life. Your focus will be getting yourself right with the Lord before you start ministering to and with others. The best way to see someone's life change is to have your life change first.

The majority of the challenges focus on real people in our lives that we can share God's love with in practical ways. Just some of the examples of the different people you will be reaching out to are your family members, lost souls, neighbors, authority figures, friends, enemies, people you look up to, people you look down on, needy people, and church members.

Days 7, 14, 21, 28 and 35: These Sunday challenges are designed for reaching out to those within your church fellowship.

Days 37–39: These challenges focus on learning how to share your faith verbally. Don't be scared or discouraged. We haven't even started yet. You'll do fine with this section. I saved it until last because I am confident you will feel better about these challenges after you have seen some "success stories" from the previous challenges.

Day 40: Here we are forced to look back at all the previous 39 challenges and write down as many testimonies as we can as a way of testifying God's power and all that He did.

Day 41 (40 Days Plus 1): This is the challenge of all challenges because it emphasizes living the rest of your life like you did the first 40 days.

At the end of each challenge is a "Testimony or Comments" section. This is for you to write down any information as a testimony of what happened after each challenge.

You will find that some of these challenges include being an encouragement to others. Some people like to buy thank-you cards or blank cards for writing their own kind words. You may want to purchase some cards ahead of time if you don't want to use the blank paper you have in your home.

You will notice that Day 1 starts on a Monday. It is set up this way because Days 7, 14, 21, 28 and 35 are challenges that relate to people you'll see Sunday at church. I know everyone is different, and you may only be able to attend church on a Wednesday night or some other day or night. If that is your case, then adjust and adapt this devotional book to your schedule.

I'm excited that you are willing to carry out these 40 challenges and look forward to what God is going to do in your life. May the Lord bless you and those around you as you move forward each day!

Day 1

Monday

When to Do My Devotions

Read Exodus 1:1–22.

SEVENTY FAMILY MEMBERS of Jacob's family, the Israelites, lived in the land of Egypt. As a new generation of Israelites arose, their numbers greatly multiplied. By this time a new king—Pharaoh—had taken over Egypt. This king was not at all a friend of the Israelites like the previous king. Instead, he feared the Israelites because of their large numbers. His plan was to make them his slaves. He put slave masters over the Israelites and oppressed them with forced labor. He made sure they were treated ruthlessly. Despite this plan, the Israelites multiplied even more. This resulted in Pharaoh ordering the midwives (the ladies who helped women deliver their babies) to kill the baby boys and let the baby girls live. Because they feared God, the midwives would not kill any babies. As a result, God blessed the midwives.

Both the midwives and Pharaoh held fear within them. Pharaoh feared the Israelites and that he would lose his power. Rather than turning to God, he chose to take matters into his own hands. He chose to treat the Israelites disrespectfully, and he became a very ruthless leader. He did not turn toward God nor pursue God with his heart. In the end it ended up hurting him and his family, while other Egyptians even lost their lives.

The midwives, on the other hand, feared God. They loved Him and respected Him. This resulted into wanting a life of obedience. They did not want to make any decision that would displease their God, despite the consequences they could have faced from Pharaoh, including death. Because they had this fear, love and respect relationship with God, they did what was right versus giving in to what the non-believers told them to do. The women had hearts for the Lord and were faithful to Him with their hearts and souls.

Read Joshua 24:14–15.

Moses and Joshua were the two leaders God used in bringing the Israelites out of Egypt and into the Promised Land. In accomplishing this great feat, God did many great miracles for His chosen people. Even after all God did, many Israelites still chose to follow false gods or turned their hearts toward the pleasures of this world instead of toward God. In this passage, Joshua is presenting before the Israelites two choices: either to serve God completely or serve other gods or things. Joshua declared loud and clear what his choice would be. He chose what the midwives chose. He chose to serve the Lord.

Read Deuteronomy 6:4–5.

Let us also ponder today who we will serve. Do we want to serve the Lord God or not? Do we love the Lord God with all our hearts, soul and strength? Or are we living in fear? Do we fear we will lose our friends or popularity? Perhaps we fear we will lose our fortune, fame or power? Our fear will either drive us away from God (like Pharaoh) or toward God (like Joshua and the midwives). Which will we do?

My prayer is that your love for God will drive you to Him, just as your love for a friend also drives you to spend time with him or her. Think about how you communicate with your close friends. For some of you, it's almost an all-day event. You find yourself texting, Facebooking, e-mailing, calling, going out with and spending time with your close friends. In reality, what greater friend could we have but the friend we have with Christ the Lord? Let's pursue Him with all our hearts by developing our relationship with Him. Okay, so we can't text, Facebook or e-mail our God, but we can communicate with Him through our prayer time; and He desperately wants to speak to us through the Word of God, the Bible. In order for this to happen, we need to set some time aside where we can be alone with God without any distractions.

My challenge today is that you will pick a time slot of each day of the week when you can have uninterrupted time with God for doing your devotions.

This is crucial because if you don't establish your time slots, then the next 39 days of your devotions will never happen. I already know some of the excuses that are being said. The biggest excuse is "I don't have time." You will use your job, your education, your busy schedule at home, and all kinds of other excuses as to why you don't have time. Trust me, I understand those excuses, and I'm not trying to be unsympathetic. I feel your pain. But as a testimony for God, I've attended school and was active in sports as well. I've worked a 70-hour weekly job, I've been to college with a busy, busy, busy, struggling work load, and I have a family as well. Among all these busy schedules, I made it a priority to spend time with my God. God is not asking me to "fit Him into my time schedule." He is asking me "to center my time schedule around Him."

How much time do you free up for your devotions? Let's free up one hour but no less than a half hour. You'll find that an hour will go very fast as you do these challenges. In order to free up some time, it may mean sacrificing some other areas of your lives. Perhaps spend an hour less time on your electronics. The average person spends four hours a day on their electronics. This may mean quitting one of your four activities after school or quitting one of your three jobs. I know, this is going to be hard, but putting God first and then working your life around Him means you can trust God to help you with your finances and every other area of your life.

I have two time charts below so you can fill in all the necessities of your life. One of them is already filled out as an example of how to do it. The other one is blank for you to do your own scheduling. If you don't want to write in the book, then get a piece of paper and make up your own time chart. What many of you will find is that the two-plus hours a day you spend on your computer or iPod is actually free time to spend with the Lord. Some of you may find that your traveling time to work or school is the ideal time to spend praying and praising God. Be creative, but have a time slot for each day that you can spend with the Lord with your devotions. Let's get started! You will be glad you did this!

You'll notice I have my devotions in the morning. I recommend that because you will have all day to live out what you have read in your devotions. However, there are some people who swear they cannot have morning devotions. Then please pick a time that will work. I have sleep time, devotion time, personal time, family time and meal times. You realize that your schedule will change some days because of unexpected situations that come up, but this will be a good guideline to follow. Now work on your time schedule and see where you can best have your devotions! Have fun!

Example of When to Have My Devotions

	Sun.	Mon/Wed/Fri	Tues./Thurs	Saturday
4:30 a.m.	Sleep	Devotions	Devotions	Sleep
5:00 a.m.	Sleep	Devotions	Devotions	Sleep
5:30 a.m.	Shower	Devotions	Devotions	Sleep
6:00 a.m.	Devotions	Devotions	Devotions	Sleep
6:30 a.m.	Devotions	Exercise	Exercise	Sleep
7:00 a.m.	Prayer	Exercise	Exercise	Sleep
7:30 a.m.	Prayer	Exercise	Exercise	Devotions
8:00 a.m.	Church	Shower, Breakfast	Shower, Breakfast	Devotions
8:30 a.m.	Church	Work	Errands	Exercise
9:00 a.m.	Church	Work	Errands	Exercise
9:30 a.m.	Church	Work	Errands	Shower, Breakfast
10:00 a.m.	Church	Work	Errands	Personal
10:30 a.m.	Church	Work	Errands	Personal
11:00 a.m.	Church	Work	Errands	Personal
11:30 a.m.	Church	Work	Errands	Personal
Noon	Church	Lunch	Lunch	Errands
12:30 p.m.	Family	Lunch	Lunch	Errands
1:00 p.m.	Lunch	Work	Cut Wood	Lunch
1:30 p.m.	Family	Work	Cut Wood	Youth
2:00 p.m.	Family	Work	Cut Wood	Youth
2:30 p.m.	Family	Work	Cut Wood	Youth
3:00 p.m.	Family	Work	Visitation	Youth
3:30 p.m.	Family	Work	Visitation	Youth
4:00 p.m.	Church	Work	Visitation	Youth
4:30 p.m.	Church	Work	Visitation	Relax
5:00 p.m.	Church	Supper	Visitation	Supper
5:30 p.m.	Church	Supper	Supper	Supper
6:00 p.m.	Church	Youth	Supper	Relax
6:30 p.m.	Church	Youth	Family	Planning
7:00 p.m.	Church	Youth	Family	Fun Time
7:30 p.m.	Church	Youth	Family	Fun Time
8:00 p.m.	Church	Youth	Family	Fun Time
8:30 p.m.	Church	Personal	Family	Fun Time
9:00 p.m.	Relax	Personal	Personal	Fun Time
9:30 p.m.	Relax	Personal	Relax	Fun Time
10:00 p.m.	Relax	Relax	Relax	Fun Time
10:30 p.m.	Sleep	Sleep	Sleep	Fun Time
11:00 p.m.	Sleep	Sleep	Sleep	Sleep
11:30 p.m.	Sleep	Sleep	Sleep	Sleep
12:00 a.m.	Sleep	Sleep	Sleep	Sleep
12:30 a.m.	Sleep	Sleep	Sleep	Sleep
1:00 a.m.	Sleep	Sleep	Sleep	Sleep
1:30 a.m.	Sleep	Sleep	Sleep	Sleep
2:00 a.m.	Sleep	Sleep	Sleep	Sleep
2:30 a.m.	Sleep	Sleep	Sleep	Sleep
3:00 a.m.	Sleep	Sleep	Sleep	Sleep
3:30 a.m.	Sleep	Sleep	Sleep	Sleep
4:00 a.m.	Sleep	Sleep	Sleep	Sleep

Example of When to Have My Devotions

	Sunday	Monday	Tuesday
5:00 a.m.			
5:30 a.m.			
6:00 a.m.			
6:30 a.m.			
7:00 a.m.			
7:30 a.m.			
8:00 a.m.			
8:30 a.m.			
9:00 a.m.			
9:30 a.m.			
10:00 a.m.			
10:30 a.m.			
11:00 a.m.			
11:30 a.m.			
Noon			
12:30 p.m.			
1:00 p.m.			
1:30 p.m.			
2:00 p.m.			
2:30 p.m.			
3:00 p.m.			
3:30 p.m.			
4:00 p.m.			
4:30 p.m.			
5:00 p.m.			
5:30 p.m.			
6:00 p.m.			
6:30 p.m.			
7:00 p.m.			
7:30 p.m.			
8:00 p.m.			
8:30 p.m.			
9:00 p.m.			
9:30 p.m.			
10:00 p.m.			
10:30 p.m.			
11:00 p.m.			
11:30 p.m.			
12:00 a.m.			
12:30 a.m.			
1:00 a.m.			
1:30 a.m.			
2:00 a.m.			
2:30 a.m.			
3:00 a.m.			
3:30 a.m.			
4:00 a.m.			
4:30 a.m.			

Wednesday	Thursday	Friday	Saturday
			.

DAY 1

Testimony or Comments:

_____

_____

_____

_____

_____

_____

_____

_____

_____

_____

_____

_____

_____

_____

Day 2
Tuesday

Finding That Place of Solitude

Read Mark 1:9–13, 35; Luke 5:15–16; 6:12–16.

Now THAT WE HAVE established *when* we will have our devotions, let's establish *where* we will have our devotions. *Who* better to look to as our example than Christ Himself!

In **Mark 1:12–13**, before Jesus started His ministry, it says that He went to the desert to spend 40 days alone. Jesus was preparing to start a major lifelong ministry and did not take it lightly. He wanted His Father to be in complete control and was willing to obey His Father. The Spirit led Him to the desert for 40 days and nights, where He went through temptations and challenges. Yet He never lost focus of God and His Word.

Sometime after He started His ministry, He had to make a decision on what men He called on to be His disciples—men that He chose had to be able to mentor, teach, train and serve as role models. In **Luke 6:12** it says Jesus went to a mountain to spend the night in prayer. The decision Jesus had to make was not to be taken lightly. He wanted the choices that He made to be God directed. I wonder just how often we go before God in prayer when we have major decisions to make.

It was Jesus' general practice or habit to isolate Himself from others and find a quiet place of solitude to pray. When we pray, it should be in a place where there will be no distractions, as Jesus did in **Mark 1:35** and **Luke 5:15–16**. Even when Christ fed the 5,000, He withdrew to be alone with God. Another time, Jesus heard the bad news about His friend John the Baptist and again went away to be alone with God. This pattern was true throughout His life. Even when He was preparing to go to the cross, He went to the Garden of Gethsemane to be alone. Sure He took His close friends with Him, but He told them to stay in a given area and pray while He went on farther to be alone and pray. All through His ministry, He taught His disciples to do the same thing, and He is teaching us to do the same today.

Where is your place of solitude? Where are you able to withdraw from people, noise, cell phones, computers, television, beepers, pagers, faxes or other stimulations of life?

My challenge is twofold: (1) Where is your place of solitude? and (2) Where do you turn when you have to make decisions?

Think about your life. What are you going through? When you have to make a decision in your life, where do you turn? Do you turn to people? Do you try to do it yourself? Let's realize that God loves us and wants to help us with every aspect of our lives. It could be related to school, our job, our occupation, our future, our family or our church. Whatever it is, God wants us to go to Him first. Don't get me wrong: in Scripture we are told that it is wise to seek counsel from others, but it doesn't say to leave God out of the picture. So let's go to God first before we jump to make any quick decisions. God is willing and waiting to intervene. Go to Him in prayer *today* with all that is on your heart.

For me personally, my place of solitude is usually in my living room sitting in my recliner. In the evening, this is a very noisy place. But in the early morning, it is a very quiet place. Once in a while, I'll take a walk down behind our township building. Both places enable me to be very open with the Lord and very attentive to His Spirit's speaking to my heart and mind. I pray you find that special place like I have found.

Tomorrow we will look at developing an actual prayer list. God bless you, and keep moving forward.

Testimony or Comments:

Day 3

Wednesday

Communicating with God

PRAYER IS A POWERFUL thing! We should not forget that. God wants us to pray and even asks us to pray. Prayer is a way of saying, "God, I recognize You are in control, so I am turning to You!"

Prayer is a way of expressing our faith. "God, I am praying to You because I believe You will work in my life situations." Failure to pray is a way of saying, "I can do this myself" or "I don't need God!" or "I don't believe God can help me in this situation." So let's be people of prayer.

Today I want to challenge you to put together a prayer list.

All it takes is a piece of paper. You can make it as fancy as you want. Your prayer list can either be handwritten or typed. Either way, create one. It will help you stay focused when you pray so you are less apt to daydream or even less likely to fall asleep.

Let's look at Scripture passages that help paint a picture of what our communication with God should look like.

PRAISE & THANKSGIVING

Give thanks to the Lord, call on his name; make known among the nations what he has done. (**1 Chronicles 16:8**)

I will praise God's name in song and glorify him with thanksgiving. (**Psalm 69:30**)

Let everything that has breath praise the Lord. Praise the Lord. (**Psalm 150:6**)

Here we see how God wants us to thank Him for the blessings in our lives. So when you go before God, take time to thank Him for the blessings of a recent answered prayer, or a blessing of an act of kindness done to you, or for your family members or friends. Anything! Even thank God for your home, food, a warm place to sleep at night. Realize that though we complain that we don't have enough "stuff" in this world, there are many who have literally nothing and even die because of the lack of "stuff." They don't have money, they don't have good health, they don't have a place to sleep, and some fight to find food. Really, do we have it all that bad? So let's take time in our prayers to say thanks to God and praise His name. I even have song sheets so I can sing songs of praise to the Lord.

SELF

If my people, who are called by my name, will humble themselves and pray and seek my face and turn from their wicked ways, then will I hear from heaven and will forgive their sin and will heal their land. (**2 Chronicles 7:14**)

Here we read that God wants us to be right before Him. So we need to humbly approach God in prayer, realizing we ourselves have areas that need to change. Let's not be so arrogant as to believe that everybody needs to change but we don't. Let's truly go before God and plead with Him to strip us of our imperfections so that we can be better used in ministering to others, knowing of course that it could be painful.

THOSE IN AUTHORITY

I urge, then, first of all, that requests, prayers, intercession and thanksgiving be made for everyone— for kings and all those in authority, that we may live peaceful and quiet lives in all godliness and holiness. (**1 Timothy 2:1–2**)

This passage instructs us to pray for those who are in authority. Who are your authority figures? Make a list of names and then pray for them. It could be your parents, your boss, your teacher, your leader, the principal, the president, etc. Put their names down and take time to pray for them.

THE BROKENHEARTED

The Lord is close to the brokenhearted and saves those who are crushed in spirit. (**Psalm 34:18**)

Here we read that God wants to help those who are hurting. We all know people who are hurting in some way. People struggle all around us. As you sit in school or in a place full of people, take a look around and just watch. Watch and see who seems to be hurting. There are people thinking of suicide, wearing masks, and we don't even know it. Some are hurting financially or looking for jobs or have broken marriages or broken relationships of some sort. Some have been rejected and feel all alone. Pray for those you know are hurting. Put their names down and keep them in prayer.

THE SICK

Then the king said to the man of God, "Intercede with the Lord your

God and pray for me that my hand may be restored." So the man of God interceded with the Lord, and the king's hand was restored and became as it was before. (**1 Kings 13:6**)

Here's an example in the Bible where God's people prayed for the sick. Do you know anyone who is sick? Put their names down and pray for them. Sometimes you learn who is sick because you spark a conversation with them and learn of their illness. If you are praying for them, then ask them a few days later how they are doing. Just think of the impact that would have on their lives. They would appreciate that you said you'd be praying for them, but they would doubly appreciate it if you ask about them at a later time. It would show you *really* do care.

YOUR ENEMIES

"But I tell you who hear me: Love your enemies, do good to those who hate you, bless those who curse you, pray for those who mistreat you." (**Luke 6:27–28**)

Here's an example where Jesus is asking us to pray for those who mistreat us. Maybe you know people who just don't seem to like you. Are you praying for them? Also, instead of letting them know of their terrible faults, think of ways to love them. Be a person who loves like Jesus does versus one who condemns. As you pray and love, you'll see changes both in your attitude toward them and in how they respond to you. List the names of those who are "enemies" or who "mistreat" you, and pray for them.

THE UNSAVED

Brothers, my heart's desire and prayer to God for the Israelites is that they may be saved. (**Romans 10:1**)

Here's an example where people prayed for those who did not know Christ as their Savior. Last but not least, think of names of those you know that don't know Jesus. As you pray for them, God will give you opportunities to share His love with them. God will work in their lives when you don't even see it. List names of those you know who don't know Jesus and pray for them.

After completing this list, take time each day to pray for some or all of the requests. You do it as you feel you should. I personally pray for something different each day, except for certain requests that I'm praying for immediate answers of some sort. It could be sick people or people who are looking for jobs or who are struggling in certain areas. Please do this and trust that God will be working in many lives.

Testimony or Comments:

_____

_____

_____

_____

_____

_____

_____

_____

_____

Day 4

Thursday

God Communicating with Us

Today read Deuteronomy 6:4–9 and Joshua 1:1–9.

HERE ARE TWO GREAT passages that deal with the value of God's Word and include commandments. In Deuteronomy, God speaks to the Israelites and tells them that the most important thing in their lives is to love the Lord their God with all their heart and all their soul and all their strength. Can you imagine that? To love God with this much intensity is ever so powerful and involves all of who we are. Do we love God that much? Is there anyone or anything we find ourselves pursuing more than God Himself?

The writer of Deuteronomy doesn't stop at just telling us how *much* to love God but gives specific examples of what our lives will be like if we really love God that much. We'll teach God's Word and commandments to our children and to our family members. We'll take advantage of every opportunity to talk about the commandments. We won't be able to *not* talk about God's expectations because they are so much a part of our lives. Have we attacked God's Word to study and learn because we want God's expectations to be a part of all we are? How important is God's Word in your life?

Look at **Joshua 1:1–9**. Moses, who was leading the people of Israel out of Egypt to the Promised Land, has just died, and God is now calling Joshua to be the new leader of all Israel. God first assures Joshua he has nothing to worry about because God says He will be with him wherever he goes. But then God instructs Joshua on the important ingredients in order to become a great leader: obey God's Word completely in order to be successful wherever you go and keep God's Word always on your lips because you never know when He may want you to speak it to someone. We also should meditate on God's Word day and night. How can we meditate on something if we are not reading it, studying it or maybe even memorizing it?

My challenge is to make reading God's Word the most important responsibility of your life on this earth.

Start studying *now* and continue until you leave this earth. I tell you from experience that as you make reading, studying and memorizing God's Word a priority in your life, God will give you a ton of resources in your heart and mind to use to impact your own life as well as others' lives. God's Word will change you and those around you.

As you step out of bed to lead your family or to be a leader at school or at work, take God's advice that He gave to the Israelites and to Joshua. Let God's Word fill you and emanate from you to others.

This challenge is to not just read God's Word but meditate on it and let God speak to you. If you do so, you'll find yourself hearing God talk to you about your own life. He'll take the Scriptures you read and make them applicable to your own life. Read a passage of Scripture more than once if you need to, but ask how what you read can be a part of your life. Then meditate on it throughout the day. Here are a couple of suggestions: (1) Take an index card and write down one major point you read that would be great to remember throughout the day; carry it with you as a reminder for the whole day. (2) Start memorizing verses. Write a "neat" verse down and memorize it. You'll be amazed at how much God will bring that verse to your mind at a most important yet unexpected moment. Try memorizing at least one new verse a month.

My goal is to get you past reading a chapter with no attempt to really try to study and learn what is really written in it. I want you to learn to stop, meditate and let God speak to you as you read. Our busy, fast-paced lives don't let us do that. We are quick to read and leave with such speed that we never let God have a chance to speak to our hearts. Have a great day with Jesus.

Testimony or Comments:

Day 5

Friday

Holy Spirit Dependent

GREETINGS! I PRAY THAT this has been beneficial to you on an ongoing basis. As you know, the focus of the first four days has been on getting acquainted with the Lord. Hopefully it has not been boring for you. Becoming His acquaintance is so crucial. We ourselves must be committed and growing in Christ before we can truly have an impact on others. Starting tomorrow, you will be challenged to reach out to those around you.

Today, however, we must remind ourselves that God is the One who will be giving us the strength to carry out the challenges, and who will be doing the changes in people's lives. We are asked to remain obedient to God and actively participate in reaching out to others. We are to love people with the love of Jesus so that we can plant seeds of Christ's salvation in their hearts or even water the seeds already there. In doing this we must remember the following truths:

1. It is God who lives and dwells within us to strengthen us and give us the ability to carry out these challenges.

2. It is God who goes ahead of us to prepare the way and the people we reach.

3. It is God who changes people's lives, not us.

If we can instill these three truths into our hearts and minds, then we can with *boldness*, *confidence* and even *excitement* move forward, knowing God is going to do a wonderful work in our lives, through our lives and into the lives of others. *Please grasp these truths!*

Let's look at each truth individually.

1. It is God who lives and dwells within us to strengthen us and give us the ability to carry out these challenges.

Read **Zechariah 4:6, Acts 1:4–8** and **2 Corinthians 3:4–5,** which are reminders that we all have the Holy Spirit as a gift when we come to know Christ. This gift is our source of power. **Zechariah 4:6** states that it is not by our might nor by our power but by the power of the Holy Spirit that we get our strength. This should be a comforting thought to us, knowing that we don't have to try so hard. We can rest knowing that God is ever present and ready and willing to work through us. We don't have to depend on ourselves for our strength, especially when we know how imperfect we are before a perfect God.

Second Corinthians 3:4–5 helps bring this truth to light in that our confidence and adequacies are through Christ toward God. Let's keep our focus on Him, knowing He supplies all we need to carry out all He wants us to do. The moment we focus on ourselves is the moment we put our trust in that which only sets us up to fail.

2. It is God who goes ahead of us to prepare the way and the people we reach.

Read **Deuteronomy 31:8** and **Joshua 1:9**. Knowing God goes ahead of us and prepares the way for His Holy Spirit to work, we don't have to be afraid, discouraged or terrified. What a comfort that is! Just as God used John the Baptist to prepare the way of the Lord, so He wants to use us to prepare the way of His Holy Spirit.

3. It is God who changes people's lives, not us.

Read **1 Corinthians 3:1–9**. As you read this passage, you see how people were bragging about certain spiritual leaders as if they were God Himself. Paul sets it straight: as followers of Christ, we are "mere" humans and "only servants." Yes, we are given responsibilities and are to labor and do His work, but our task is to share the love of Jesus with those around us, which will in turn impact people's lives. However, it is God and only God who will make people change and grow. Our jobs are important, and we will be rewarded for our acts of obedience, but when it comes right down to it, we are nothing compared to the greatness of God and what He is capable of doing.

The challenge today is certainly one we will want to do every day before we set out into the world to do God's work. The challenge is a prayer.

You can say the prayer listed below however you want to, but say it with your heart. Say it like you mean it—because you do mean it. It will open the door for God to work in and through you. It will open the door for your *boldness*, *confidence* and even *excitement* as you do God's Work.

Prayer: "*Dear Lord, thank You that even though I am a mere human being, You choose to use me. May Your Holy Spirit empower me today to love others. May Your Holy Spirit go before me and prepare people to have an encounter with You through me. Lord, change the hearts and lives of those who encounter You today. Even though I*

may not see the change, I know You are at work. Thank You. In Jesus'
name, amen!"

Testimony or Comments:

_____

_____

_____

_____

_____

_____

_____

_____

_____

_____

_____

_____

_____

_____

_____

_____

Day 6

Saturday

Get Rid of It—NOW!

Read Psalm 119:9–11 and Hebrews 12:1–3. Today is GET RID OF IT Day! There are several messages we could preach from these passages, but for today I want to talk about focusing on Jesus. God is calling us into a pure and holy life. Another word in the Bible that is used is *sanctified*, which means to be "set apart." When God talks about us being sanctified, He is asking us to be "set apart" from this world. Our life style, our life choices and decisions should be different than that of the world. Sin in our lives should become less as we are pursuing hard our relationship with Christ.

What is difficult is that Satan is fighting for our souls (**1 Peter 5:8**). He does not want us to have a relationship with Christ or to be pure, holy or sanctified. As Christians we must recognize these temptations that are placed before us and do whatever is necessary to keep away from them. For example, a teen Christian asked me to be his accountability partner. He downloaded onto his computer the software program called x3watch. This is a software program that monitors the websites you visit. If you visit a questionable pornographic site, it sends an e-mail to the two or three people you chose to be your accountability partners. He has done so well since he has started.

One day I got an e-mail. The website in question had filthy language songs. I confronted him on it, and it changed his life. The same thing happened with an adult who has me as his accountability partner. He was on a pornography site and was embarrassed to have me talk to him. He avoided my e-mails asking him about it. Ironically God caused us to run into each other at the school. There was no running away. Our interaction was positive, uplifting and encouraging. As a result, it helped him get back on track, and he has done great ever since. The website offering this software is www.x3watch.com. They offer a free version and a paid version.

Being holy, pure and sanctified means you have to recognize what the temptations are and then get rid of them or stay away from them. But it is not enough to just get rid of a temptation; you also have to replace it with something, and that is God's Word. Let's look at the passages you read.

Psalm 119:9–11

Verse 9 says, *"How can a young man keep his way pure? By living according to your word."* It doesn't take a theologian to figure this verse out. Staying pure involves knowing God's Word and then choosing to live by it. Knowing God's Word is not enough. You have to want to live by it as well. Verse 10 says it great: *"I seek you with all my heart."* How hard are you seeking God? How bad do you really want to live according to His Word? The rest of verse 10 says, *"Do not let me stray from your commands."* God knows it won't be easy, but we must look to Him for strength and help. We must pursue and seek Him daily and surround ourselves with Christian friends so we are not easily tempted away from God. Are you putting yourself into compromising positions which will make it difficult to stay focused and pure?

Being in God's Word and making it a part of our lives means we can fight against sin as stated in verse 11: *"I have hidden your word in my heart that I might not sin against you."* So what should be done with those temptations we encounter? **Hebrews 12:1–3** addresses this issue. In verse 1 it says, *"Let us throw off everything that hinders and the sin that so easily entangles."* What do we do? We get rid of it! Then once we get rid of it, we must keep the faith by persevering and not giving up. We keep our eyes focused on Jesus, who will help us. He knows what we are going through and will help us not grow weary and not lose heart, as mentioned in verses 2 and 3.

 Challenge of the day: Identify and find anything and everything that causes you temptation, and get rid of it.

Go through your home and bedroom, computer, iPods, music, vehicle, cell phone, books, games, clothes and, yes, even your relationships. I realize this is going to be hard. But how bad do you want Jesus, and how bad do you want to be pure, holy and sanctified (set apart)? Remember "to get rid of" is not enough. You must replace it with your heart pursuing God, His Word and Christian fellowship. My prayer is that you will do what is necessary to be set apart with God!

Testimony or Comments:

_____

_____

_____

_____

_____

_____

Day 7

Sunday

STOP Showing Favoritism

TODAY IS THE DAY we start focusing on others rather than ourselves. I'm excited about this because I have witnessed how much these small acts of kindness impact other people's lives. Sometimes I find that as I "impact" someone's life, I go away feeling impacted as well or even growing closer to the person to whom I reached out. The people that we will be reaching out to throughout these coming days will be family members, church family members, neighbors, classmates, teachers, school administrators, bosses, coworkers, enemies, friends, and who knows what other surprises.

Read James 2:1–10.

This passage basically says not to show favoritism. It talks about how people in church see the popular people and often are drawn to them, reach out to them and want to be around them. But when a not-so-popular person comes to church, they ignore them. Sometimes they are outright rude about it. These unpopular people leave the church feeling totally rejected and find themselves hating "church people" or "Christians" in general; to them, Christians come across as selfish, hypocritical people. As a result, they never come back and often end up hanging out with those who do show them acceptance and love. Oftentimes the non-Christians who are partying and making bad decisions are the ones that welcome them into their "family" of people. It bothers me to think that non-Christians sometimes do better at accepting the unpopular people than the Christians do. I'm just as guilty as the next person.

 Sunday's challenge is to reach out to someone in the church who doesn't really get a lot of attention.

Sit back and pray to God to show you who He would have you reach out to. This could be a youth or an adult. It could be a whole family—maybe a family that shows up for the first time or has been there for a while but it seems no one has connected with them. Take some time to talk with the person God lays on your heart, or shows you, or puts right smack dab in front of you. Talk to them and introduce yourself. Find out what they like to do. Invite a youth, adult or family to lunch after church at a local restaurant (depending on your budget). You could even invite someone to a home-cooked meal.

You could also reach out to one of the elderly in the church. They love the attention and would appreciate anything you do for them. Giving a hug, taking cookies or a card to one of them would make them feel good. Tell them you will be praying for them this week, and ask if they have a prayer request. I have seen great results with this. I'm serious! This would put such great joy in their hearts. It will bring joy to your heart as well.

Hey sport lovers! You could invite someone to one of your afternoon activities. There are so many different ones to choose from: basketball, football, softball, kickball, video games, Ping-Pong, foosball, air hockey, board games, etc. Even invite them to Sunday night church and give them attention so that when they leave they feel like the most important person there.

Have fun with this.

Testimony or Comments:

Day 8

Monday

Lost Souls

A LEADING JEW NAMED Saul lived in Jerusalem after Christ's death and resurrection. He was a well-educated man and did his best to destroy the Christian church after Pentecost. He even participated in the killing of Stephen, the first Christian martyr (**Acts 7:55–8:4**). Saul, who had several men with him, traveled to Damascus so he could find and imprison more Christians. While traveling to Damascus, Saul met the Lord. He repented and turned in faith to Jesus Christ. After this experience, he changed his name to Paul. Then he went from trying to destroy Christians to trying to persuade Jews and Gentiles to become Christians.

Paul was committed to this task and ended up going on three separate missionary journeys—each several years in length. Paul preached the news of Jesus in many coastal cities and trade route towns. As a result, he was faced with many challenges and hardships, but he did not give up. Seeing lost souls come to Christ was so important to Paul that when he faced hardships, he persevered. He would not give up. If rejected in one area, he would go to another area.

Read the passage below and see all that Paul went through.

2 Corinthians 11:23b–28

I have worked much harder, been in prison more frequently, been flogged more severely, and been exposed to death again and again. Five times I received from the Jews the forty lashes minus one. Three times I was beaten with rods, once I was stoned, three times I was shipwrecked, I spent a night and a day in the open sea, I have been constantly on the move. I have been in danger from rivers, in danger from bandits, in danger from my own countrymen, in danger from Gentiles; in danger in the city, in danger in the country, in danger at sea; and in danger from false brothers. I have labored and toiled and have often gone without sleep; I have known hunger and thirst and have often gone without food; I have been cold and naked. Besides everything else, I face daily the pressure of my concern for all the churches.

Wow! The man went through so much, and after all was said and done, he ended his statement with the fact that he still had a concern for the churches (for souls). Paul had a *vision* to see lost souls come to Christ, he was willing to obey *God's plan* to reach lost souls and he was *committed* and willing to *persevere* despite the hardships he faced.

VISION: Does your heart hurt for the lost? Do you have a vision to see lost souls come to Christ? If you answered yes, then pray for God to lay five people who need Jesus as Savior on your mind. Then write their names down. Pray for them each day, and pray for God to open the door for opportunities to reach out to them with God's love.

GOD'S PLAN: It is not enough to just have a vision. You also need a plan. When God had a vision to rescue the Israelites out of Egypt and take them to the Promised Land, He had a plan by which to accomplish it. His plan was to use Moses as the leader. Moses was to listen to God and obey His plan. This is the same with God's vision to bring forgiveness of sins for all humankind. His plan was to send His Son, Jesus, who was also obedient to God. God has also given us a plan to reach lost souls around us, as stated in **John 13:34–35**: *"A new command I give you: Love one another. As I have loved you, so you must love one another. By this all men will know that you are my disciples, if you love one another."*

On a regular basis, we should be creative in ways we could reach out to the five people we listed. Just do acts of love or acts of kindness. In doing so, you will establish a stronger relationship with them. This is important so that on the day God opens the door of opportunity for you to share Jesus verbally, you can do it knowing your friend will be more apt to listen to you. They may reject your message but will respect you and your position because of how you have been treating them.

COMMITMENT and PERSEVERANCE: If you are serious about this, you'll keep praying for those five people and keep doing acts of love to and for them. If they totally reject you, then just be a person that respects them. Don't force a message on them, but let your life be the message. Jesus said if you love them, they'll know you are a Christ follower.

Here is today's challenge (some of you may already be doing this, but if not, this will help you): List five names of people you know who don't have a relationship with Jesus.

1. _____

2. _____

3. _____

4. _____

5. _____

Pick one person that you can do an act of kindness to as a way of showing God's love. You can do something for them—bake cookies, cook a meal, buy a meal for them, pay for their meal at school lunch, compliment them, encourage them if you feel they need it, give them a ride to a destination, send a card. My favorite is inviting them to your house for a game night (this is great when you invite other Christians as well). You don't bombard them with a Jesus message; you just have fun as a team. After a while, you'll see that you will be able to invite them to a church event or even share your own testimony. Perhaps you may feel already connected with them, so you may want to invite them to a Christian event that the church is doing. Pray and do something!

Thanks, and persevere!

Testimony or Comments:

_____

_____

_____

_____

_____

_____

_____

Day 9

Tuesday

Point Your Family to Jesus

GREETINGS! TODAY'S FOCUS will be your family. Please read **Acts 16:16–40**. This is one of my favorite stories in the Bible. I have heard many sermons about Paul and Silas who were thrown in jail. But as you read this, take your time and think about the jailer in charge of the prisoners. Put yourself in his shoes (sandals) and try and capture the thoughts going through his head. You may even want to read this passage twice and let God speak to you about what is going on.

Now that you have read the passage, let's get a quick overview of what has happened. Paul and Silas have been traveling and preaching the thoughts and teachings of Jesus. While in the city of Macedonia, they begin going to the place of prayer. They are met by a slave girl who has a demon in her who predicts the future. She follows Paul and Silas for days and becomes very annoying. This slave girl is very popular among the people, because people are constantly paying her to tell their future.

In the meantime, the slave girl's owners are making a ton of money from her predicting. Can you guess what happens when Paul casts out this demon in the name of Jesus? The owners lose a great deal of income and are furious! They have a powerful influence among the magistrates (leaders of the city) and make horrible accusations against Paul and Silas. The people of the city are also angry because they lost the person they depended on for predictions. The city joins together against Paul and Silas, and they are stripped, beaten, flogged and then placed into the most inner part of the prison.

Now we come to the story about the Roman jailer who is in charge of Paul and Silas and the other prisoners. The Roman jailer is given strict orders—rather, he is *commanded*—to guard them carefully. Now let me put this into perspective. As a Roman guard or jailer, if any prisoner was to ever escape, it meant you were killed for failing to do your job. So when this jailer is commanded to guard them carefully, he goes to great pains to make sure they will not get away. He takes Paul and Silas to the most inner cell. This is the deepest cell in the cave. He not only locks them into the jail but locks their feet into the chains. He is making it extra certain they will not get away.

While in prison, Paul and Silas begin praying and singing praise songs to God. The Lord at this time does a miracle! He sends an earthquake, which opens all the prison doors and loosens all the shackles from all the prisoners. This means all the prisoners could escape! The Roman jailer awakens from his sleep and assumes all the prisoners have escaped. Can you imagine what must have gone through his mind? He thinks the prisoners escaped while he was asleep, and then he fears having to explain to his authorities what has happened. He knows he is in big trouble so he grabs his sword to kill himself.

Paul, realizing this, shouts and stops the jailer by saying, "We are all here!" This results in the jailer falling before Paul and Silas and asking them what he must do to be saved. The jailer is not the only one who accepted Christ. His whole family did as well! What a change in this jailer's heart. He was once *so* concerned about keeping them in prison but is now more concerned about the spiritual aspect of life. He takes them out of prison and to his house. What he once valued as most important has now been replaced by a new passion—a new priority. We see several things happen that night.

1. He takes them home so his whole family can hear about Christ.

2. They take care of Paul and Silas's wounds instead of being disrespectful to the men.

3. The whole family is baptized, signifying a commitment to live for Jesus.

4. They feed Paul and Silas a meal. (The jailer is feeding the prisoners! Isn't that wild?)

5. Lastly, it says the jailer is "filled with joy"! To see himself and his family now in a relationship with the Lord Jesus is an extremely joyous event.

It was not enough for the jailer to be saved; he wanted his whole family to be saved. He wanted it so much that he violated every Roman prison law and took the prisoners out of jail and to his home. To be caught in this act would mean the death penalty for the jailer. But the spiritual well-being for his family was so important that he was willing to make the risk. But as you read the rest of the chapter, you see that everyone returned to their regular positions before daylight.

How much do we want Jesus in our lives, and how much do we want Jesus in the lives of our whole family? If it is important to us, what are we doing to help this happen? What risks are we willing to make?

My challenge is that you would do something that would show you care about the spiritual well-being of your family and do something that lets them know that their spiritual well-being is important.

For example: If you are from a Christ-believing family, take the risk of calling your family together and have a devotional together with prayer. Stress to them in your devotional how important it is to have a growing relationship with Christ. Give them a chance to share any prayer concerns or troubles. Share this devotional with them if you want. Who knows, this may lead you to buy a devotional book that you can read with your family once a day or once a week or once a month. If you are not comfortable with reading a devotional, then take the risk of getting your family together and say you want to have a time of prayer with them. Pray for each other's needs, or pray that their relationship with Christ would be a growing relationship. Then stress how important it is to do things to keep growing in God's Word, in prayer and in fellowship. Do something! Ask for God's direction.

If you are from a non-believing family and you know they would not be ready for a family gathering of Bible time and prayer, then you can go through your house and go from room to room praying for the spiritual well-being of each family member. Ask for God to use you to show the love of Jesus. Pray for opportunities to actually share the love of Jesus. Pray and do something; it will have an impact. Trust God even if you get resistance. Don't be overly pushy, but take a risk and see what God does.

DAY 9

Testimony or Comments:

Day 10 *Wednesday*

Spiritual Hero

Today is Spiritual Hero Day, which involves contacting someone who has inspired you or impacted your life in some way. People who have influenced you probably sometimes feel like they are not doing a "good job" and would appreciate some kind of feedback. One year I Googled my discipleship leader in college and tracked her down. I called her and thanked her for her spiritual inspiration. It took time to locate her—a lot of time—but it was worth it. I remember she was very appreciative.

Here we go. Read 2 Kings 4:1–7.

The wife of a man from the company of the prophets cried out to Elisha, "Your servant my husband is dead, and you know that he revered the Lord. But now his creditor is coming to take my two boys as his slaves." Elisha replied to her, "How can I help you? Tell me, what do you have in your house?" "Your servant has nothing there at all," she said, "except a little oil." Elisha said, "Go around and ask all your neighbors for empty jars. Don't ask for just a few. Then go inside and shut the door behind you and your sons. Pour oil into all the jars, and as each is filled, put it to one side." She left him and afterward shut the door behind her and her sons. They brought the

*jars to her and she kept pouring. When all the jars were full, she said
to her son, "Bring me another one." But he replied, "There is not a
jar left." Then the oil stopped flowing. She went and told the man of
God, and he said, "Go, sell the oil and pay your debts. You and your
sons can live on what is left."*

Let me paraphrase this passage: This woman's husband used to
be a prophet along with other prophets, and for some reason he
died and the wife was left with two sons. She cried out to Elisha, the man of God, because she was in turmoil. Because her
husband had died she was unable to make enough money to
pay her bills, and the debt collectors had been knocking at her
door to collect the money. Finally they told her that the next
time they came they would take her two sons as slaves for their
full payment if she did not have the money. So the woman cried
out to Elisha in desperation. He asked her a question: "What
do you have in your house?" He was looking to see if she had
anything of value in her home. She at first said she had nothing
but then remembered the little bit of olive oil she had in her jar.

Though the woman had very little of it, olive oil was a valuable source of wealth in the days of King Solomon (**1 Kings
5:11; 2 Chronicles 2:10**). Oil had been used for a great variety
of purposes in Bible times. It largely took the place of butter
in eating. For cooking purposes, it was used in place of animal
fat. Ezekiel mentions three important items of diet: oil, flour
and honey (**Ezekiel 16:13**). Olive oil was also used for light in
lamps. The most famous example of this is the "ten virgins who
took their lamps and went out to meet the bridegroom" (**Matthew 25:1**). Olive oil was often used for anointing the body
(**Ruth 3:3**). Finally, oil was commonly used in various religious
ceremonies. It formed a part of the meal offering (**Leviticus
2:1**). The prophet was anointed with oil when he took over his
duties (**1 Kings 19:16**). The priest was also anointed with oil

when he took over his duties (**Leviticus 8:12**). The king was anointed either by a prophet or by a priest (**1 Samuel 16:13; 1 Kings 1:34**).

Knowing its value, Elisha told the woman and her two sons to collect as many jars from all their neighbors as possible. The more the merrier. They were then instructed to fill up the jars with olive oil from the only jar of it she had. A miracle occurred, and she was able to pour out the oil in an unlimited fashion. Oil continued to flow out of the jar until *all* the jars were full. She was then instructed to sell the olive oil; since it was in such high demand, she was able to sell it all. She made enough money to pay her debts and have enough left over for her and her two sons to live off of.

I'm sure the woman was full of gratitude and saw Elisha as her spiritual hero. How appreciative she had to feel knowing her two sons would not have to be slaves to another family. She went from a place of mental distress to a place of great joy!

What about you? Who has been influential in getting you from a place of distress or sin to a place of joy and salvation? Or who has been influential in helping you grow in your faith?

Who is that one person (or persons) who has been your spiritual hero? I challenge you to take the time to give that person a note, or call them on the phone, or go to them in person.

However you decide to do it, let them know how appreciative you are.

Have a blessed day!

Testimony or Comments:

_____

_____

_____

_____

_____

_____

_____

_____

_____

_____

_____

_____

_____

_____

_____

_____

Day 11

Thursday

Thanks for Making a Difference

Read Acts 3:1–10.

A S YOU HAVE READ this passage, you see two of Jesus' closest followers heading to the temple for their normal three hours of prayer. This incident occurred just a few days after Pentecost—the time when the Holy Spirit was poured out on the disciples and apostles of Jesus. Peter and John had been filled with the Holy Spirit and were committed to doing God's Work. As they walked to the place of prayer, they met a crippled man who had been collecting money at the temple gate for years. This meant everybody had seen and known this man. He was begging for money, and as Peter and John approached him, they recognized that he had a need greater than money. They wanted him to have and experience Jesus in his life. Peter and John could have just walked by the man and not given him another concern. They could have even thrown a coin in his basket and kept right on going, but they didn't. They took the time to stop; they recognized his need for Jesus; and in faith they said, "What I have I give you."

Peter's prayer for Jesus in this man's life became evident through the miraculous healing that took place. This greatly impacted this man—he was walking, jumping and praising God. Even people who saw him afterward were in awe and amazement. The rest of chapters 3 and 4 reveal how the name of Jesus spread throughout the land and was glorified by this incident.

Let me ask you a question: Who is someone you know that reminds you of Peter or John? Who is someone you know that you see impacting people's lives? They may have never done anything for you, but they have done so much for others. They take the time to stop and help others. They are making a difference in people's lives.

 Your challenge is this: Take the time to thank this person for how they demonstrate God's love in other people's lives.

Do it by card, phone call, with a gift, or some other creative way. I put a banner up in someone's yard once saying, THANK YOU FOR MAKING A DIFFERENCE. Whatever you do, *thank them!*

Now, this may sound weird, but if this person is not a Christian, you could do the same thing with a little twist. For example, I ran cross-country back in the 1970s and I still remember the coach for one of our opposing teams in Pennsylvania. He also remembers me. He is a great coach with great success. To be as successful as he is means he has to invest greatly with those he coaches. I heard that his school district recognized him for his 40 years of service. I don't know if he is a Christian, but I had a plaque made honoring him for his 40 years of service and mailed it to him with a card. I wish I had an exact copy of what I said, but the gist of it was I wrote a little about the "good old days" of running and told him what I was doing now. I mentioned a passage in the Bible about how Christ impacted lives so they could one day have a relationship with Him and spend eternity in heaven. I then mentioned how great it was to see how he had invested his life in others for so many years and how I was certain he had impacted them in many ways. I wrote, "I don't know if you are a Christian," and I included a little challenge in the card about how he could have that same relationship with Christ like those who Christ impacted in the Bible. I'm not sure that he gave his life to Christ, but I know a seed was planted.

Pray for the Lord's leading, and He will help you!

Testimony or Comments:

Day 12

Friday

Shock Your Parents

TAKE THE TIME NOW to read **Ephesians 6:1–3, Colossians 3:20** and **1 Timothy 5:3–8**. For some teens, these passages do not seem to exist in the Bible. These passages emphasize obedience and the honoring of the very ones with whom teens often find themselves in conflict. However, if the first two passages were put into practice with a good attitude and a good heart, I strongly believe there would be fewer problems between teens and their parents. To get to this point means having to get over the "steep hill" of selfishness. For some, it is difficult to let go of immediate selfish pleasures so we can obey and honor our parents. Our parents ask us to do something, and we want to *wait*—and we expect our parents to wait with us. We would rather selfishly watch TV, be on the computer, play Xbox 360 or be with our friends.

Today's challenge is the shock challenge! It's called shock challenge because today you are going to shock your parents by doing your daily responsibilities without being asked.

But don't stop there; go above and beyond your daily responsibilities and *really shock* them by doing one other chore that you are not usually asked to do. For example, if your daily chores are to take out the garbage, clean your room, clean up your shoes, pick up clothes lying around the house, and hang up your coat, do these things without being asked. Then when you're finished, go and do something that would be totally unexpected. For example, vacuum the carpet in the living and dining rooms, dust the furniture in two rooms, set the table, clean off the table or wash the dishes.

Then when your parents come to after fainting and ask why you are being so nice, tell them today is Honor and Obey Your Parents Day and you want to show your love for them. At that point, maybe it would be a good idea to hug and kiss your parents and tell them you love them.

If you are an adult who no longer lives with your parents, then this is where **1 Timothy 5:3–8** comes in. This passage does not say *honor* or *obey*, but it is a great example of how it is important to honor and show respect to our parents and grandparents. Parents and grandparents often get lonely and long for a visitor. Why not take the time to visit them? Or if distance is an issue, then send them a very nice card and/or call them on the telephone. If your parents are no longer alive, then think of those one or two individuals who have been a mother or father figure in your life. They have role modeled what it means to be a great mother or father. I'd like you to show honor or respect to them by writing to them or sending them a card expressing some kind of thanks for their impact on your life. You don't have to say thanks for being a mother figure or father figure to you (unless you want to), but write words that express your gratitude for their influence on your life.

Have fun with this challenge, and have a blessed day!

DAY 12

Testimony or Comments:

_____

_____

_____

_____

_____

_____

_____

_____

_____

_____

_____

_____

_____

_____

_____

Day 13 Saturday

Love Your Enemies

READ MATTHEW 5:43–48, Luke 6:27–36 and Romans 12:9–21, and as you read please do the following: Find a piece of paper and a pencil or pen and make two columns. As you read, write down in one column every positive thing the verses say we should do in regard to our enemies; and in the other column, write down everything they say we should not do.

Before looking at your two columns of answers, first let me ask, "Who is your enemy?" Your enemy is anyone who opposes your viewpoints or behaviors, such as your spiritual convictions, your work ethics, your morals, your decisions, etc. In fact, the Bible says in **Matthew 10:34–36** that your enemy may even be the members of your own household. This is especially true if you are a believer in Christ and they are not. Everything you live for or everything that defines who you are in Christ opposes their life choices, values and beliefs. Some cannot even stand to be in your presence because of the conviction they feel when around you. On the other hand, some cannot stand to be in your presence because they feel so unloved when they are in your presence.

Today's devotion focuses on how we are to treat our enemies.

Study over your two columns of answers. See any patterns? Notice any similarities from one passage to the next? Here is what I came up with:

LOVE ENEMIES is mentioned four times.

DO GOOD TO THEM is mentioned four times.

TREAT THEM AS IF THEY ARE BETTER THAN YOU is alluded to three times.

PRAY FOR THEM is mentioned two times.

LEND TO THEM is mentioned two times.

GIVE TO THEM is mentioned one time.

EXPECT NOTHING IN RETURN is mentioned two times.

BLESS THEM is mentioned two times.

GREET THEM is mentioned one time.

TREAT THEM AS YOU WANT TO BE TREATED is mentioned one time.

TURN THE OTHER CHEEK is mentioned one time.

BE MERCIFUL TO THEM is mentioned one time.

ASSOCIATE WITH THEM is mentioned one time.

GET ALONG WITH THEM is mentioned one time.

LIVE AT PEACE WITH THEM (as best as you can) is mentioned one time.

FEED THEM & GIVE THEM DRINK is mentioned one time.

BE SINCERE is mentioned one time.

DON'T GET REVENGE is mentioned two times.

DON'T CURSE THEM is mentioned two times.

DON'T WITHHOLD FROM THEM is mentioned one time.

DON'T DEMAND BACK is mentioned one time.

DON'T DO EVIL TO THEM is mentioned one time.

If we do not take to heart these very inspired words of God, then we will miss a great opportunity to impact and change our lives and others' lives. Please meditate on your two columns. Let God speak to you as to how He can use you to minister to an enemy. Don't be surprised if God tells you to do these things several times over several days. Personally, I can give two examples where I did something good and loving to an enemy; I received two different responses.

Once, a student and I gave money to a very angry and hateful teen as a way of reaching out to him. This brought an immediate change in his heart in how he treated us. Another time I did acts of love and kindness to a student, and it seemed nothing was working. His disrespect toward me seemed ongoing. I mention this because sometimes we pick and choose who we will love and who we will seek revenge on based on how we *think* they will respond to us. God asks us to love our enemies—*period*. There is no criteria defined on picking and choosing who we should show love to and who we should seek revenge on. We are expected to love all our enemies regardless of how they respond to us or regardless of how we think they will respond to us.

Let me say this as a caution. There may be times when an enemy violates us in a way that requires outside help (police, counselor, teacher, principal, etc.). That does not mean we hate them; it just means that sometimes this outside intervention is what is needed to truly help someone get on the right path.

The challenge today is this: What can you do to show love to your enemy?

This love you may display is something you may be doing for quite some time. Be patient. Don't let your frustration or their responses break you down to revenge or cursing. For example, a father's son was his own enemy because the son did not want a life with Christ. This hurt the father deeply, and he found himself correcting and confronting his son every time the son visited him. It got to the point where the son quit coming around. This taught the father to love the son despite their differences when they were together. The son *knows* what his dad's convictions are. The father realized he did not have to keep reminding the son. The father learned, and is continuing to learn, to show love to the son, and it has helped their relationship. His prayer is that his ongoing love to his son will one day result in the son coming back to the Lord.

Do you realize the patience and perseverance and self-control that is needed to make this work? Is that not a picture of God with us? Let us then also be patient, persevering and showing self-control as we love our enemies. Let us turn to the power of the Holy Spirit for His help. Blessings to you!

Testimony or Comments:

_____

_____

_____

_____

_____

_____

_____

_____

Day 14 *Sunday*

Touch the Heart of a Widow

Read James 1:26–27.

I N THIS PASSAGE OF James you just read, we see James addressing a problem in the church. There were people who felt they were pretty "religious." Perhaps they were followers of Christ in the early days and later became a little prideful about their faith. They began exalting themselves above others and giving the impression that they were better than others. As a result, they became blinded by what was really happening in their lives. They had acquired foul mouths. They were probably saying bad words and gossiping about others instead of encouraging others and helping others.

In their own minds, they were *super spiritual*; but because of their mouths, God said their religion or faith was "worthless"! Ouch! Can we relate with that? Do people see the love of Jesus coming out of our mouths or even from our lives in the way we treat them? Or have we also gotten to the point where we think we are so much better than others that we don't have to scoop downward and help them? This passage is very short, but James grabs ahold of our prideful little hearts and pulls us downward and points us where our focus must be—on the lowly hurting people. God says in this passage that religion or faith that is acceptable is looking out for widows and orphans in their distress. We need to get our attitudes and hearts in the place where we see others as better than ourselves and not as below us. Once we do that, nothing will stop us from continually reaching outward.

Your challenge for today is focusing on the widows and widowers of the church.

Take some time to talk to a widow or widower of the church. Perhaps you can invite him or her to lunch after church at McDonald's or Perkins (depending on your budget). Make a snack and write a card, and give them to a widow or widower on Sunday. Let them know you have been thinking of them and wanted to do something nice for them. Widows and widowers go through something many of us just don't understand—losing a loved one that was a major part of their lives, and they now have a huge hole in their heart that needs healing and mending. Your love and attention can help do that. Once again, many blessings. And thanks for staying focused on your devotions!

Testimony or Comments:

_____

_____

_____

_____

_____

Day 15

Monday

Respect Authority

BEFORE YOU READ TODAY's passage, let me give you some history leading up to this chapter. King Saul was anointed by God to be king over Israel. After David had killed Goliath, he went from being a shepherd in the field to becoming a great warrior for Israel. In fact, his popularity became so great that King Saul grew very jealous of David and tried to kill him several times. Saul, along with many men, even pursued David to attack him, overtake him and kill him. Twice David had an opportunity to kill Saul, but out of respect for Saul's position as king, he chose not to. Despite the fact that King Saul was trying to kill David, David still wanted to show respect for his authority—the king.

The last chapter of 1 Samuel gives the final accounts of Saul's life. Israel is in a heated battle with their enemy—the Philistines. David is not in this battle, but the news comes to him about Saul's death. There! Now you can read today's passage.

Read 2 Samuel 1:1–16.

Now that you have read this passage, let's not focus so much on what David did but more on why he did it. Three days after Saul's death, a man reached David to give him the news. The man was in terrible shape. He fell before David in respect and told him that Saul and his son Jonathan were dead. This man, an Amalekite, told David that Saul tried to kill himself by falling on his own spear but was still alive and was being pursued by the enemy, the Philistines. Saul did not want to fall into the hands of his enemy, so he told the Amalekite to kill him. So the man did.

David always had the attitude that the position of king was a position of authority established by God, and this position should always be respected. To show any kind of disrespect would be such a horrible act of sin. So horrible that David saw it as worthy of death, which is what happened to the Amalekite man. Meditate on the fact that if God establishes a position, then the position should be treated with utmost respect.

Was Saul acting in a manner worthy of respect? No, of course not! He was trying to kill David out of jealousy. How respectful is that? But David set an example for us to follow. Respect shown to a person in authority is not something we do when they respect us first. God does not ask us to respect our authority figures when they are respectful to us. He asks us to show respect because He put them in the position of authority. We are to respect those in authority because they have authority over us—not based on how they treat us.

First Peter 2:13 says we are to respect "every authority instituted among men"—those who treat us well and those who seem to enjoy punishing us. So let me ask, who are your authority figures? They could be your boss, your parents, your teachers, your principal at school, the administration at the school, the president of a club you are involved in, your coaches, the older gentleman or woman who is your neighbor and seems to enjoy yelling at you when you step on their property. Whether these authority figures treat you positively or negatively, they are to be respected by you!

Your challenge today is to show one or more of your authority figures some form of respect.

(Don't choose your parents since you have already honored them in a previous challenge. Pick some other authority figure.) Write a note that lets them know how much you appreciate them. Perhaps you need to apologize for past disrespectful behavior. A card and cookies are always a nice gesture, but not necessary. A note of some sort is nice in that it is a constant reminder of how they are a blessing. When someone writes something nice about you, you often refer back to what was written. Don't assume others don't do the same. Your note could come at such a vital moment in their life. God would use your note as an encouragement. After you express this form of respect, let it become a part of your thought process and a part of your behavior so that your authority figures see this respect permeating from your life every day and not once in a great while.

Take the time to do this. Pray first for God's leading and wisdom for the right act and right words. Have fun and trust God will use it for His glory!

Testimony or Comments:

Day 16

Tuesday

Forgiven

READ MATTHEW 27:26–31, LUKE 6:37, Matthew 6:14 and Matthew 18:21–35, and read them in the order listed here. Jesus went through so much for us so that our sins could be forgiven. I mean, think about it. Jesus did nothing wrong. His crime was He loved people and helped them. He was a threat to the so-called religious leaders who were jealous of His popularity. Their jealousy hindered their ability to see Jesus as the person He claimed to be: the Christ, the Savior of the world. The religious leaders did everything they could do to kill Jesus—but they never could. But at the right time, Jesus willingly let them arrest Him; and on His own free will, He let them abuse Him physically and verbally. They flogged His body 39 times with a whip with sharp objects at the end. His flesh was literally torn open so that you could see His bones. He was slapped and punched in the face. His head was repeatedly beaten with a club. His body was so bruised and swollen that the Bible says He was unrecognizable. He was mocked and ridiculed, spat on, made fun of, humiliated before the crowds of people and forced to carry a cross of a criminal when in fact He committed no crime. Then they nailed Him to that very cross, where they ridiculed Him even more. Before Christ died, He cried out to His Father and said, "Father, forgive them, for they do not know what they are doing" (Luke 23:34).

Hebrews 9:26 and **1 Peter 3:18** say that Christ's death was sufficient to bring forgiveness to everyone. The question is, do we want to accept it? His death was not just for those who nailed Him to the cross, but even for all of us today. There are days we say things or do things that deny Christ or mock Him. I guess you could say in some ways we are no different than the so-called religious leaders. They denied Jesus! Don't we do the same thing when we make decisions that hurt Him or violate His laws? This love is so great from Jesus that as we accept His forgiveness, our sins are remembered *no more*, as stated in **Hebrews 8:12** and **10:17**. We do not deserve the love of Jesus or His forgiveness, but because of His love, grace and mercy, we receive that which we do not deserve.

This Jesus, who has gone through so much and has still forgiven us, wants us, by His power and love, to forgive others. He asks us to forgive those who "don't deserve to be forgiven" because He lovingly forgave us when we didn't deserve it. This is *so* important that Jesus said (as you read in **Luke 6:37** and **Matthew 6:14**) if we don't forgive others, then He won't forgive us. That seems to be a very harsh statement. In fact, as you read in **Matthew 18:21–35**, you see how harsh of a punishment that awaits those who don't forgive. *Why is that?* It is because when we are filled with *forgiveness*, then we are filled with *love*.

Forgiveness enables us to experience healing in our bodies and souls. Seriously, to harbor unforgiveness is to be filled with hate. Our thoughts are hateful toward the ones who have wronged us. We condemn them, judge them and speak badly about them. We do the very thing we don't want Jesus to do to us. Whenever we think about them, we are filled with anxiety. This anxiety, if not dealt with, will cause stomach problems and even ulcers, or worse yet, put a strain on our hearts. This doesn't happen overnight but will eat at us, and the long-term effects can be physically dangerous. Then, of course, let us not forget about the spiritual consequences.

Sometimes we are so hurt by what someone does to us that we conclude his or her sin against us is *not* worthy of forgiveness. I understand that, and so does God. He understands our hurts and pains. Remember, He has gone through it. He knows that you *can't* forgive some people. That's why He wants to help you so you can. He can give you the love that is needed to say, "I forgive you." We can't do it on our own. When we get to that point, healing will begin to occur in our own minds and bodies. Don't let the sins of others keep you from being all God wants you to be. If you forgive, that does not mean your relationships with those who wronged you will be restored (it could happen, but it may not). But it does mean you will be freed to move onward and forward with Christ in a growing relationship.

 Challenge of the day: Who has wronged you or hurt you? Identify who this is and let God help you forgive them.

For some, this is a one-step process. You call them up or write a letter, or approach them face-to-face and let them know you love and forgive them. But for most people, it is a process of time. We need to spend limitless time in prayer, asking God to fill us with His love toward others so we can begin to prepare for the act of forgiveness. How do we do this? If someone hurt you, communicate to them what they did and how it hurt you. As you talk with them, you may learn something about them you never knew which would give you a better understanding as to why they did what they did. Not that what they did was okay, but because you understand it, it gives you more of a heart of grace and mercy. You may find that they did not realize how much they hurt you. In that sense, you experience healing in the relationship because both of you talked about it.

Perhaps the person who wronged you has died. Then write on a piece of paper all your pain, frustration and hate, then lay it before God and begin to pray for His help to say, "I forgive you." You may go to a grave site and speak to the site as if you are actually speaking to the person. Speak your heart as if you are speaking to the person in front of you. Say, "I forgive you!" God will then bring healing to you so you can move onward. The person who wronged you may not be receptive to you at all, and in that sense, it is like they are dead. Then write on paper again all your pain, etc., and lay it before the Lord. Tell God you forgive them, and then be praying for this person, that God would heal their heart as well.

I realize that this is a difficult challenge. As a counselor of teens who have been verbally, physically and sexually abused, I know how difficult it is for them to forgive others and therefore know how difficult it may be for some of you. At least take the first step by asking for God's help. God bless you!

Testimony or Comments:

Day 17

Wednesday

Humility

Today read Philippians 2:1–11 and Romans 12:10.

I F THERE ARE THREE WORDS to describe this devotion, it would be *humility*, *servanthood* and *honor*. What does it take to be "great"? Or, I should say, what does it take to make others strongly feel you are "great"? There is a difference. In our minds, feeling "great" means having power, money, things or popularity, or being a leader of a large group of people. Often being "great" in our own minds means having "things" people can see on the outside. They go by your house and see how big it is or see the expensive clothes you wear or even how much money you carry around in your wallet. These are things we can see, and in our minds we have become "great"! On the other hand, there is a "great" that draws people in, and they admire you not because of what they see on the outside but rather what they see on the inside. They see a person of *love* and *integrity*. They see a person with *humility* who *encourages* others and makes them feel good. You build the self-worth of others. You are always trying to do for others. "Great" people are people of great *character*.

Who great people are on the inside becomes so beautiful that the legacy they leave behind is not the cars, houses, clothes or large bank accounts. Their legacy lies in the memories of the people they have helped—maybe they helped someone learn to drive a car; or they volunteered time to help fix someone's house; or they gave up clothes so someone who had none could have some; or they offered money to someone for food, sacrificially giving from their wallet so the other person could eat. Let me please clarify that if people have a lot of "stuff," this does not mean they are automatically "bad" people. A small percentage of people have been blessed with material things and have used it for the glory of God. But to look at Scripture, it says a person with a lot of stuff has a hard time staying focused on God. The message today is not how much money and stuff you have but rather what kind of a person you are on the inside. I would like us to look at the person who is our best example to follow—Jesus Himself.

As you read **Philippians 2:1–11,** you see the character qualities that Jesus had are the very qualities the Bible is asking us to acquire or obtain. Verse 1 says if we are united with Christ, meaning we have a relationship with Him, then the qualities He had will over time become who we are. We will be people of love who comfort others. We will fellowship with others and show tenderness and compassion. The things we do will not be motivated by selfishness or selfish gain, but we will be motivated with a very humble heart toward others so that we will consider others better than ourselves. The lives we live do require us to think of our own interests, but a person with Christ's humility also goes outside their own world and looks to the interests of others. We learn not to get so "locked" onto our own needs that we lose focus of those in need around us.

Jesus was so willing to take His eyes off of Himself and onto the world's problem of sin that He left His heavenly position of power so He could become a man on earth. He actually became more than just a man. He became a *servant*. He humbled

Himself from being on the throne in heaven to a lowly stable and later became a servant. The passage asks us to be just like Jesus: humble servants who are looking outward versus inward so we can impact the lives of others. God asked Jesus to do this, and Jesus was obedient to listen to His Father. He was obedient even to the point of giving up His life for *us*! In doing so, He received a great reward. What is our *character*? If people evaluated me, would there be a long list of names who would say, "Blair impacted my life!" "Blair was not a selfish person!" "Blair helped me in my need!" "Blair was a great example of a *humble servant!*" Or would they be saying just the opposite?

Today's challenge is to be a humble servant who impacts the life of another.

Wait! We want to do this keeping in mind **Romans 12:10b**, where it says *"Honor one another above yourselves."* I don't want you to reach out to just *anyone* but to the person who you feel is *below* you. It does not take much humility to honor someone that everybody loves to be associated with. Let's do this Jesus' way and honor someone we think we are better than or above, and honor them like they are Jesus Himself. If we are going to be humble servants of God, then we can't look at people as if they are below us. We must train ourselves, with the help of the Holy Spirit, to look at others as if they are above us. What person today could you reach out to and make them feel really good, important and valuable?

Last year I gave thank-you cards to the three crossing guards in our town. I felt that was the most humiliating job. So I treated them like they had the best position ever. I wrote such a nice card to each one. Now, every time they see me, they vigorously give me a wave. Do something today. You might be surprised at the responses.

Testimony or Comments:

_____

_____

_____

_____

_____

_____

_____

_____

_____

_____

_____

_____

_____

_____

_____

_____

_____

Day 18

Thursday

Neighbor Day

Read Matthew 22:34–40.

THIS PASSAGE IS a great one to memorize (or at least verses 37–39). The teachers of the Law were tempting Jesus. They hoped to cause Jesus to say something inappropriate so they could accuse Him of wrongdoing and get rid of Him. Jesus in turn responded with such great wisdom that instead of making Himself look bad, it made the teachers of the Law look bad. When asked which commandment was the greatest, Jesus responded that the command that says we are to love the Lord our God with all our heart, soul and mind is the greatest command. But the second greatest command is to love our neighbors as ourselves. Meditate on Jesus' response. What are we doing and saying that shows we love God more than anyone or anything?

But let me ask you this as well: What are you doing that shows you love your neighbors? You know how busy we are. It is difficult to get everything done that *we* want done. We prioritize and work on things that will benefit us and not our neighbor. We tell ourselves, "Today is a busy day." We have sports after school, homework, our job, cleaning in the house, cooking, house chores, computer time, TV time, cell phone time, etc., etc., blah, blah, blah! We prioritize that which is important to *us*. How often do we make it a part of our daily or weekly schedule to do something nice for our neighbors? Can you name all the neighbors that live on each side of you? When was the last time you reached out to them in some way? I'm guilty as sin! I admit that this is one of my weaknesses.

Today's challenge is to connect in some way with your neighbor.

Go to one of them and see how they are doing. Maybe you'll see them working outside. Go over and talk to them. Go over and help them with their work. Go over and do a job that you see needs to be done. Our neighbor mowed our lawn for us one week while I was gone. I appreciated that! Our youth primed and painted our neighbor's house for them. What a way to connect! Maybe your specialty is not talking, or maybe you are not able to do manual labor but you love to cook (not me)—so bake some cookies or, better yet, make a meal for a neighbor. When you fix or cook your supper or lunch, make enough to feed the husband and wife across the street, and take it over to them.

When they ask why you did it, tell them that it seems people just don't do enough for each other in the neighborhood and that it's your way of saying thanks for being your neighbor. Or say you just wanted to be nice. These are great ways to plant seeds of love. Doing these simple things may one day result in being able to share your faith in Jesus. That's what it is all about. Don't just think about your neighbors as people to be nice to, but think of them as souls who need Jesus. Doing acts of kindness for them opens the door to share your faith.

Have fun!

DAY 18

Testimony or Comments:

_____

_____

_____

_____

_____

_____

_____

_____

_____

_____

_____

_____

_____

_____

_____

_____

Day 19

Friday

Thank You Friend(s)

READ THE FOLLOWING: **Matthew 17:1–3, A Special Moment:** *After six days Jesus took with him* **Peter, James and John** *the brother of James, and led them up a high mountain by themselves. There he was transfigured before them. His face shone like the sun, and his clothes became as white as the light. Just then there appeared before them Moses and Elijah, talking with Jesus.*

Mark 5:35–37, For Ministry

While Jesus was still speaking, some men came from the house of Jairus, the synagogue ruler. "Your daughter is dead," they said. "Why bother the teacher any more?" Ignoring what they said, Jesus told the synagogue ruler, "Don't be afraid; just believe." He did not let anyone follow him except **Peter, James and John** *the brother of James.*

Mark 14:32–34, A Time of Distress

They went to a place called Gethsemane, and Jesus said to his disciples, "Sit here while I pray." He took **Peter, James and John** *along with him, and he began to be deeply distressed and troubled. "My soul is overwhelmed with sorrow to the point of death," he said to them. "Stay here and keep watch."*

Mark 13:3–4, Hanging Out and Talking

As Jesus was sitting on the Mount of Olives opposite the temple, Peter, James, John and Andrew asked him privately, "Tell us, when will these things happen? And what will be the sign that they are all about to be fulfilled?"

Though Jesus loves the whole world, He still had certain disciples that He seemed close to. In Scripture we see that in certain times of His life, He was hanging out with specific people, not a whole bunch of people. The three most common people were *Peter, James and John.* Jesus was no different than the rest of us when it comes to friends. Though we like a whole bunch of people and maybe have many friends, when it comes to doing something special, we seem to most often pick the same two to four friends to spend that special time with.

Think of the times you seem most often to call on one, two or three special friends. Maybe it is your vacation or going to a movie or getting a quick bite to eat. Perhaps it is when you are going through a very difficult time. See, Jesus is not much different. As you read the passages above, you see where Jesus called on His closest friends during a special moment, during ministry time and during a time of great distress. He was also with them for no particular reason other than just to hang out.

Challenge for today: Think of those friends you are most close to, those one to four friends you hang out with the most, and take time today to let them know how much you love them and appreciate them.

Do this with just your mere words if you want. Or if you are more creative, take a picture of a friend (from Facebook or from your collection of pictures) and put it on a piece of paper; then under the picture, write: "Ten things I love most about my friend." List those ten things. Perhaps you will buy a cute little gift and give it to them with a card. Everyone is different, but you should take the time to do something. You never know how long God is going to allow you to be together.

I remember when a local teen boy shot himself and how devastating it was for the whole community. He was a football player, and I'll never forget at the funeral standing beside two of his teammates. One of them was crying and said, "I never told him I loved him." I realize some teens and adults have a difficult time saying, "I love you"; they find it easier expressing their love in other ways. However you choose to express your love and appreciation, just make sure you do it in a way so that you have no regrets later on.

Thanks for your love and commitment in doing these devotions.

Testimony or Comments:

_____

_____

_____

_____

_____

_____

_____

Day 20

Saturday

Honor Authority

Read Esther 2:21–23 and 6:1–11.

AFTER READING THESE passages, let me say that you should make a note to read this whole book. It truly is one of my favorite Biblical accounts. You can't really appreciate what happened to Mordecai without reading the previous passages. King Xerxes was a king of 127 provinces. He was well known and very powerful. He and his people were not friends of the Jews nor did they have a close relationship with them. However, as you read **Esther 2:21–23**, you see that Mordecai (the Jew) was hanging out at the king's gate. While at the gate, he overheard how two of King Xerxes's guards were conspiring to kill the king. This troubled Mordecai, so he reported it to the queen, who reported it to the king, which resulted in the two men being punished by death.

King Xerxes's life was saved by Mordecai the Jew. Regardless of the fact that Jews were not considered friends among the king and his people, Mordecai, out of respect for the king's authority, reported this conspiracy. What is somewhat comical about this Biblical account is the fact that King Xerxes's most favored man, Haman, really hated Mordecai the Jew. When Haman entered the king's court, everyone bowed down to Haman; but Mordecai never bowed down to Haman because Mordecai would bow to God only. Because this infuriated Haman, he had a plan already set up to have Mordecai killed. Isn't it ironic that at that same time King Xerxes was reminded of the day when Mordecai saved his life? When the king realized that Mordecai was never properly rewarded for his act of respect, he decided to honor Mordecai. And isn't it ironic that it ended up being Haman who took Mordecai around the city so Mordecai could be honored?

How does this Biblical account tie into our challenge today? Regardless of how much you are "liked" or not "liked" among those in authority, you are to show them utmost respect. You do it out of love and respect for them—not because you want something in return. The motives must be proper. What is neat to see here is oftentimes something happens when we show respect for those in authority over us. It often results in them having an increased respect for us. They end up thinking we are "okay." They tend to never forget your acts of respect, and this could result in a blessing for you later on down the road. Again, you don't show respect with the motive of getting it back. You show it because you are supposed to, but realizing that some of the benefits could be getting it back. In fact, it may come back to your advantage at a time you really need it.

Mordecai the Jew respected the king and expected nothing positive in return. But when the king chose to honor Mordecai, it came at a time when Mordecai was close to being killed by Haman.

Your challenge today is to show honor or respect to your authority figures.

Students, choose to show respect to your principal or to one of the staff members in the administration building. Perhaps you would want to make three or four dozen cookies with a note saying thanks for all they do and give it to all the staff in the administration building. We have had a group of teens send one thank-you note to the district superintendent expressing their appreciation for all he has done. We once did the same for the principal of the school. Imagine how they must feel to receive such a note. If you are doing this challenge during the summer, then look up the address of your principal or district superintendent and send them a note stating your appreciation and letting them know you are praying for them. Seriously, how often does a school staff person get a thank-you note in the summer? Not very often! You would certainly make their day.

For you non-students, choose your boss, a board member, the CEO, or the plant manager. A simple note can do much. Any other gifts you present on top of that is up to you and your creative mind. If you are self-employed and have no "boss" because you are your own boss, then think of the board members or elders of your church. How often do they get a thank-you card? God can give you the name of the person that could best use a thank-you card. Send it expecting nothing in return, but know it will bless them and one day maybe even bless you back.

Testimony or Comments:

_____

_____

_____

_____

_____

Day 21

Sunday

Thank You Church

HAVE YOU EVER HAD SOMEONE do something for you and, either because of being busy or just plain wrapped up in your own world, you forgot to tell them thank you? I remember as a child I had a Captain America doll . . . er, I mean Captain America *action figure*. He was by far my favorite action figure. He had the rotating arms you could raise up or down. But you couldn't go sideways with them. One unfortunate day, the hook inside Captain America's body came unhooked from one of his arms. Could I get that back on? It was so difficult. I'd try and reach inside the body and grab the hook, and then I'd have to pull it outside the body far enough to rehook it. The spring tension on the hook was so tight it was almost impossible to get it out far enough. Well, my dad was very willing to help me with it. He tried everything but had a difficult time as well. Finally he got needle-nose pliers and reached in and pulled the hook outside the body. The sad thing was that the needle nose was in the way of being able to slip the arm back on. My dad fought and fought with trying to get it on. Eventually my dad grabbed the hook with his fingers in hopes of being able to slide the pliers down far enough to make enough room for the arm. However, when he released the pliers, the tension on the hook pulled back so quickly it ripped some of the skin off his finger. I remember it started to bleed. My dad quit so he could get a Band-Aid. It was getting late, and my mom said it was bedtime. It was a disappointing night. I went to bed while Captain America still suffered with a missing arm.

I remember waking up in the morning and seeing on my footboard a fully attached, two-armed Captain America. It is hard to explain the joy I had to see him all back together. I was so excited! I jumped out of bed, grabbed my action figure, ran down the stairs, and hugged and thanked my dad. There was great excitement. I don't know how he did it, but he did—and I was grateful!

When someone does something kind for us, it's amazing how we can either be very thankful people or give no response. When we neglect to thank someone, it's almost as if we feel we deserve what we got or we think what they did is not all that significant and doesn't merit an expression of gratitude. Sometimes we are so selfish in our thinking that we forget about the blood and sweat that went into the act of love. Don't get me wrong: when we do an act of love for someone, the Bible does say not to expect anything in return. However, as far as being the recipient of the act of love, we should express some kind of gratitude.

Read Luke 17:11–17.

This story is about ten men who all had leprosy. Leprosy is a bacterial disease that damages different parts of the body such as the eyes, nose, earlobes, hands and feet. It results in skin lesions and deformities, which greatly disfigure the parts of body. Those with this disease were outcasts and considered "unclean" people; those without the disease would not associate with them at all. Jesus, however, saw these men who plead for His pity. He responds to them and tells them to go show themselves to the priests. What is interesting about this statement is that it was a common practice to show yourself to a priest if you thought you were healed from leprosy. The priest would then examine you and determine if indeed you were or were not healed. So when Jesus told them to go to the priests, He was, in essence, telling them they would be healed.

Sure enough, on their way to the priests, they were healed. Although all were healed, only one was respectful enough to return and show Jesus his appreciation and give praise to God.

My challenge is that I want us to be thankful people to God and to the leaders of the church!

It's Sunday, and within the church are many ministries for children, youth, young adults and older adults. Many people put forth a lot of love, time and sacrifices to help see lives changed. Today in church, take the time to thank the different leaders of the different ministries. There are children's Wednesday night leaders, junior church leaders and workers, Sunday school teachers, older adult ministry leaders, choir directors, elders, trustees, deacons, music ministry leaders, childcare leaders, academy leaders and, of course, the senior pastor and youth pastor. But usually the other leaders get less recognition for what they do, so be sure and thank them in a special way today. It could be something verbal or something that takes a little more time, such as a card, a telephone call or a small gift. Then take time to pray for the leaders and thank God for them.

Praise God, but thank the leaders.

Testimony or Comments:

_____

_____

_____

_____

_____

Day 22 *Monday*

Parent-Child Relationship

Read Genesis 15:1–6 and 22:1–19 about Abraham and Isaac.

IN READING GENESIS 15:1–6, we see that Abraham was child-
less. He and his wife Sarah had no children to carry on their
name and no one to take on their inheritance (their life belongings). This was very bothersome to Abraham; he was so
concerned that he said to God, *"So a servant in my household
will be my heir."* A *servant*!

It was not that Abraham hated his servants, but in those days
it was very humiliating to have a servant be the person to take
over your inheritance (or belongings). A man was to have a son!
But God quickly assured Abraham that the servant would not
be the heir but that Abraham would indeed have a son—and
not just *a* son. The number of offspring that would come from
that one son would be countless. Verse 6 says Abraham believed what God said. God promised Abraham that he would
have a son, who would one day have a son, who would one day
have a son, so on and so on, till the number of offspring would
be countless. That thought was locked into Abraham's mind.
He believed in God.

At the age of 100, Abraham had his son with Sarah his wife. Can you imagine the love he must have had for his son because of having to wait so long? They probably did so much together, in fact everything together. I say this because in **Genesis 22:1–19**, God tested Abraham to see if his love for his son was greater than his love for God Himself. God asked Abraham to sacrifice his one and only son as a burnt offering on a certain mountain. Does that not sound *crazy*? Why would God ask Abraham to kill his son as an offering? What is also crazy is that Abraham was willing to obey God and do it.

Hebrews 11:17–19 explains why Abraham was willing to do this.

1. He remembered God promised that Isaac, his only son, would continue his family. So how could God permanently kill his son if Isaac would continue the family?

2. Abraham was obedient to God because he knew God would raise Isaac from the dead so as to carry out His promise.

Abraham was so certain Isaac would continue to live that he told his servants with him, *"Stay here with the donkey while I and the boy go over there. We will worship and then we will come back to you."* We will leave and we will come back. He did not say, "Just I will return," because he had faith in God's promise. This same faith was shown after Isaac asked where the lamb for the sacrifice was. Abraham told his son, *"God himself will provide the lamb."* So Isaac went with his dad without fighting and arguing. He trusted his dad. He trusted his dad so much that he willingly let his dad put him on the altar and tie him there. He didn't scream and kick and fight back.

You may know the rest of the story. God stopped Abraham

from killing his son and did provide a real lamb. The two went back together with the servants just as Abraham believed they would. God saw that Abraham did indeed love Him more than anything or anyone else, including his own son. What a great role model for his son!

Now what does this have to do with a parent-child relationship? Isaac is certainly not the main character of this Bible passage, but if we observe him in this passage, we can learn a lot about how to love our parents. Not once is there mention of any resistance from Isaac. He was willing to *spend time with his dad* on a six-day journey. He was willing to *trust his dad* when Abraham said that God would provide. He was willing to *obey his dad* when asked to be bound on the altar of death. These are three things lacking in father-son relationships today. Sometimes it is the father's fault and sometimes it is the child's fault. Sometimes it is both.

 Parents, the challenge for you today is to schedule a one-on-one time with each of your kids.

Mom or Dad, it is great to spend time with the family together, but it is also good to have one-on-one time as well. If you have several kids, then it may take a month to complete this challenge. Pick an activity to do with your kid based on their likes or hobbies. For example, go fishing, go to a movie and ice cream, go to the park, go for a ride, go spotting for deer, go hunting, go shopping, play games with them at home alone. Do something! But while you are doing something together, make sure there is an opportunity to share with them from your heart. Share how much you love them. Share what positive God-given qualities they have and how these qualities will be used one day to impact lives. Encourage them! Let them know you are always available.

Children, the challenge for you today is to schedule a one-on-one time with one parent (or stepparent or guardian) and later with the other parent (or stepparent or guardian).

Also pick something that you think both would enjoy. If doing something is too expensive, then pick an activity that requires little or no money. If you have a job, then treat your parent. But spend time together and make sure there is an opportunity to share with them from your heart. Think of three things you can compliment them on. Thank them for being a great parent and give an example of that. Point out certain traits they have such as being a good listener, encouraging you a lot, or being a great provider—anything that would encourage your parents, just as you would want to be encouraged.

For both challenges, if you feel the relationship is a strained relationship, then use this time to apologize for not working harder at obeying them or not working harder at spending more time listening to them. Or make amends on a fight that you had by saying you are sorry or that you forgive them. This time together is *not* "let's argue and fight." It should be a time to express love, encourage each other or restore what has been broken. I know for some of you, your parent (and maybe even your child) will not do this. Prayerfully make an attempt, and if they "shoot" the idea down, then write a note to them expressing your words of compliment or encouragement or apology, or whatever you feel could be said in a card that shows love, encouragement or restoration.

For those of you who have no parents or no children, instead plan an activity with that one person you have connected with who you love like a parent or like your own child. It will be a great time and will be uplifting and beneficial for both of you!

DAY 22

Let God lead this challenge, because for some of you it will be a difficult one. But God can bring positive results. Many blessings to you all!

Testimony or Comments:

_____

_____

_____

_____

_____

_____

_____

_____

_____

_____

_____

_____

_____

_____

_____

Day 23

Tuesday

No Recognition

Read 1 Corinthians 12:1–31.

IF I'M GOING TO WATCH a sport show on TV, it is usually football. I enjoy the sport and like a good competitive game, except if it is with my favorite team—then I want them to win big time! It's less stress on my heart. However, when I was eight or nine years old, I used to go with my grandparents to the car races in Erie at the Erie Speedway. They would take the grandkids, and we would have a blast! We eventually knew the names of most of the car drivers and what number car they drove. We identified number fifteen as the dirty driver or the cheater. The car we liked the most was driven by Mr. Blackmier (that may not be how he spelled it). We all liked him and would get excited when one of his races was going on.

One night, during break time at the race track, a gentleman walked over to the flagman and was talking to him. He wasn't in the flagman's box but had his hands on the outside of the entrance. My grandparents said, "Hey, that guy talking to the flagman is Mr. Blackmier! Why don't you kids go over and get his autograph." Wow! That's all I had to hear! My heart was just pounding, and the excitement was overwhelming. I had no pen and paper for Mr. Blackmier to sign, and I remember Grandma wrestling in her purse to find a piece of paper and a pen. I watched the flagman and Mr. Blackmier talking and was afraid I would get there too late.

When Grandma finally found a little piece of paper (and I mean a little piece) and a pen, I grabbed that quicker than the rest of the siblings and ran off to get Mr. Blackmier's autograph! Can you imagine the excitement? As I ran and got closer and closer to the flagman box, I saw Mr. Blackmier enter the flagman's box. I knew if I didn't get there quick enough, he would exit the box down onto the track. Once he did that, I would no longer have any chance of getting his autograph. I ran harder and my heart pounded faster. My adrenaline was going, and I knew I was not allowed into the flagman's box, but nothing was going to stop me. I ran that far, and I did not want to give up that quick. It must have been the grace of God, because I arrived at the flagman's box just as Mr. Blackmier grabbed the pole and was ready to exit the box down onto the race track.

I remember running into the box and grabbing Mr. Blackmier's arm and yelling, "Can I have your autograph?" He turned around, looked at me, looked at the flagman, smiled, then took my pen and my little piece of paper and signed it for me. I got Mr. Blackmier's autograph! I got it! I ran all the way back to my grandparents almost as fast as I had run to get the autograph. I was so excited. I waved the autograph in the air as I returned to my seat. I gave it to my grandparents, and they both looked at it and realized the man who signed it was *not* Mr. Blackmier at all. In fact he wasn't even a race car driver. He was some "no name" worker for the speedway. Well, let me say, I was disappointed. Everyone else thought it was pretty funny. I did *all* that work for nothing, or didn't I?

In the Bible passage you just read, it states that God has given everybody a gift. Every gift is given by the Holy Spirit. Think about that! The Creator of this world has given us gifts to be used for His glory and for the common good. As believers in Christ, we all have gifts and we all make up one body, that is, the body of Christ. God makes it clear that every gift is important. All too often, we place value on the ones that we see most often or hear most often. The great evangelist becomes the "important" one and not the guy or girl who cleans up after the evangelist. The singer becomes the "important" one and not the one who got the microphones ready beforehand.

Read **1 Corinthians 12:22–26** again and let God speak to you. The passage explains how we are to treat each member of the body of Christ. It says we can't say to anyone, "I don't need you!" In fact, the ones that seem to have the gifts of lesser value are the ones we are to treat with special honor. The Lord even says to give them greater honor because He wants to make sure that there is never division within the body of believers. So just as we would get excited about the special speaker or special singer, so we are to get equally excited about the custodian and the person setting up the microphones. Or better yet, let's go with this example: just as we get excited about the race car driver, so we should show that same excitement for the guy who works at the race car grounds. I wonder how that guy felt? I have to laugh now, but really, it probably made him feel pretty good, and he probably shared that moment with a lot of people.

> **Our challenge today is to get excited about someone who has a position that seems to be "less important" but in reality isn't.**

We want that person to feel like the most important person ever. It could be a secretary, a librarian, a cafeteria worker or custodian. Sit back and think who that might be for you, then how about writing a thank-you card to them? If you really want them to feel good, get a poster board, decorate it nicely, put some nice thank-you words on it and have a bunch of people sign it. If someone else made some treats, that would be nice also. Let your imagination get as wild as it wants. The goal is to make them feel like the most important person. Remember, they are important. I'll bet it will make their day and will be something they remember forever.

Testimony or Comments:

Day 24 *Wednesday*

No Electronics

Read Luke 6:12–19.

WHERE IS YOUR CELL PHONE this morning? Did you remember it? You keep it on your nightstand right? You don't want to miss anything. You never know when one of your friends may want to get ahold of you. You hear the tone of your cell phone or hear it vibrate on the wooden stand, and you can hardly wait to grab it and see who it is. You crawl out of bed, and as you walk into the bathroom your cell phone is in your right hand. Remember, you don't want to miss anything. In fact, it goes with you everywhere you go. You have it during all your meals; it stays on your lap while watching TV or visiting with a friend. It's at work with you and even with you when you are shopping or getting groceries. It's almost as if you can't live without it. You might say, "Oh yes I can! I can live without it!" Okay, if that is true, why is it that last time you accidently left it home either you had to call your parents and ask them to bring it to you or you made sure you turned around and got it?

Look, this lesson is not about "bashing" cell phones. It's a piece of metal and plastic. I have a cell phone and as a youth pastor find it an extremely great tool to communicate a message to several teens at one time without having to spend a great deal of my time calling each one individually just to remind them to bring a snack to our youth event. But at the same time, I have gotten caught up in conversations that consumed so much of my time that I ended up neglecting time with my God, my wife or my kids, and yes, even my work. That could be said about many other things. TV can consume our time along with watching movies or listening to the radio, iPods and CDs. Video games are often addictive. Our computers can consume hours of our time. We e-mail, Facebook, Google, check sports galore, participate in fantasy football, watch YouTube, etc. Electronics are not evil in and of themselves just as spoons are not evil. Electronics don't "make" people neglect their priorities just as spoons don't make people overweight. It's more about the condition of our hearts. It's more about the *choices* we *choose* to make.

What do you want to see God do *in* and *through* your life? The fact that you are reading this makes me believe there is at least a small desire within you to grow in your faith and see God work in and through your life. The question is, what are you willing to *do* to *get* there? Great runners don't just become great runners. Great football players don't just become great football players. Great cooks don't just become great cooks. Great chess players don't just become great chess players. They have to work at it. They practice! They *invest time* in the very thing they want to grow in and excel in. That is true about our spiritual lives as well. Great men and women of God did not just become great men and women of God. They invested themselves and *time* into the very things that would help them *grow* and be *equipped* so God could use them more and do great things *in* and *through* their lives.

As you read **Luke 6:12–19**, you see how Jesus went up the mountain and prayed all night with His Father. Jesus could have prayed anywhere He wanted, but He chose the mountain because He wanted to get away from all the distractions of life. He knew how important it was to spend that *time* with God. He didn't take his Xbox 360 with Him or His cell phone, His iPod, His TV . . . Okay, you understand what I'm saying. So even though Jesus lived among the distractions of life, He was wise to know how important it was to not be consumed by those distractions and *chose* to invest His time with God. In doing so, He grew, He obtained knowledge and He opened the door for God's Spirit to work through Him. Let's look at these three points more closely.

1. **He grew.** Remember how I said great runners don't just become great runners? You grow in the area you invest in. It is the same with your faith. You grow in your faith as you spend time with the Father whether through prayer, reading the Bible or Christian fellowship.

2. **He obtained wisdom and knowledge.** In the Luke passage, you see Jesus had several disciples (or followers), but He had to choose only 12 to mentor as mentioned in verse 13. "*When morning came, he called his disciples to him and chose twelve of them.*" How in the world did He know which 12 to choose? When you spend time talking to God, He will give you the wisdom needed so you can make tough decisions.

3. **God's Holy Spirit works through His life**. In **Luke 6:17–19**, we read of the great things God did through Jesus. Lives were impacted! People with diseases were healed, people with evil spirits were cured, and power was coming from Him. It's not the words that came from Jesus in His prayer that made Him great for God. It was the condition of His heart. From His heart came the words of hunger and passion for God which God responded to.

Your challenge today is to have a no electronics day.

Now I understand your job may require you to use your cell phone or you may need your computer for homework. Apart from that, let today be a day to eliminate electronics. But don't *just* eliminate electronics; as you isolate yourself from them, spend that time with God with a heart of hunger and passion. Use this time to pray, read more of God's Word or meditate on Scripture. For example, the time you would have spent on the computer now becomes time you spend with God. If you go out the door today and forget your Bible, pretend it is your cell phone and go back and get it. I am confident that as you do this challenge more often, you will have testimonies to share. Your life will change and the lives of others will be impacted.

Testimony or Comments:

_____

_____

_____

_____

_____

_____

_____

_____

_____

_____

Day 25

Thursday

Love the Unloved

Read Luke 19:1–10.

THIS PASSAGE IS A QUICK read but is filled with great guidelines for loving the unloved. This is an area where I feel Christian people have failed terribly. We are to hate sin, but all too often we are quick to hate and condemn the sinner and condemn them. We hate and condemn them with our words, our looks and our actions. It goes against everything that Jesus did. **John 3:16** says Jesus loves everyone and brought salvation to everyone. Then verse 17 says He did not come to condemn people but to save them. Our sin will bring condemnation on ourselves. If we choose to refuse the gift of Jesus' love, then we will bring condemnation on ourselves. If condemnation comes to all who reject Jesus, then our job as followers of Christ is to reach out to the lost in a way that will entice them to want to come to Christ. Why condemn them? They are already condemned by their own sin.

How in the world are we to treat people so that they would even consider Jesus let alone accept Him as their Lord and Savior? The Zacchaeus story, along with other stories in the Bible, demonstrates what we can do. Let's look at this passage.

Luke 19:1–3 says, *"Jesus entered Jericho and was passing through. A man was there by the name of Zacchaeus; he was a chief tax collector and was wealthy. He wanted to see who Jesus was."*

Try and picture in your mind what is taking place here. Jesus was passing through Jericho. Why? What was His purpose? What was His goal? Now let's look at verse 20, which answers these questions. It says Jesus came to this earth to seek lost souls and to save lost souls. Before we can understand and appreciate all that happened in verses 1–7, we must understand Jesus' mind-set and goal. In everything that Jesus did or said, in the back of His mind and in the front of His mind, He looked for opportunities to love people to the Lord.

Can you grasp this concept? Jesus was walking to Jericho! Are you with me so far? Jesus was walking to Jericho, but in His mind He was thinking how He could love someone in a way that they would want to give their lives to the Lord. Isn't that profound? Can you imagine what this world would look like if all Christians walked with that same attitude and mind-set? It blows me away and reveals my selfishness.

All too often we are so wrapped up in our own lives and how we can benefit ourselves that we forget about the lost soul we walk by every day. I wonder what stories about me would sound like. *"One day when Blair was driving to work, he saw one of his coworkers who was hated and not respected by the community. As he drove by, Blair was thinking of all the work he had to accomplish and he paid little attention to the young man."* Or would the account look like this: *"One day when Blair was driving to work, he saw one of his coworkers who was hated and not respected by the community. As Blair's car approached the young man, Blair pulled over and rolled his window down. He kindly asked the young man if he wanted a ride to work."*

Or how about this story: *"One day as Blair was walking down the hallway of his school, he came toward a student who professed to be a homosexual. As Blair passed by him, he gave the student a dirty look. He wanted that student to know he was a sinner and was going to hell."* Or would the account go like this instead: *"One day as Blair was walking down the hallway of his school, he came toward a student who professed to be a homosexual. When Blair saw him, he made sure he said hello to the student. Later at lunch, Blair asked if he could sit with him. Blair looked at him through the loving eyes of Jesus because the student was a sinner and Blair wanted him to come to Christ and not go to hell but to heaven."*

When Zacchaeus heard Jesus was coming into Jericho, he wanted to see Jesus. He was observing Jesus to see what He was really like. He was wondering if the stories he heard about Jesus were true. Can you imagine how Jesus could have blown His testimony if He would have given the hateful, dirty look to Zacchaeus? Zacchaeus would have thought what non-believers think today: *"That Jesus person acts like he is so much better than us."* Jesus' arrogance would have made Zacchaeus feel unloved, and Zacchaeus would have wanted nothing to do with Jesus. Instead Jesus does something right in front of a large crowd of people. Jesus says to Zacchaeus that He wants to hang out with him. Jesus did *not* care what others thought. The crowd was muttering in disgust because Jesus was hanging out with a sinner. Jesus was not all about a "popularity contest" like we are. He was all about seeing lost souls get saved. His approach was to love them and invest time in them. He never accepted their sin! He hated the sin and loved the sinner. Jesus demonstrated this in the story found in **John 8:1–11,** where Jesus defended a prostitute in front of the religious leaders who wanted to stone her to death. After the leaders left, Jesus asked the woman if there was anyone else left to condemn her. She said there was no one, and Jesus said, *"Neither do I condemn you . . . Go now and leave your life of sin."*

See, Jesus loves the sinner but hates sin, and He wants people to repent or turn from sin and follow Him. That is exactly what happened with Zacchaeus. He turned from his sinful ways, and the money he stole was returned to those he cheated. That day Zacchaeus found salvation!

Jesus's mind-set is salvation of souls. We are to follow His example and love sinners, spend time with them but never accept their sin. Too often Christians spend time with sinners and end up doing the same sin. They get pulled down instead of pulling the sinner up to Jesus.

 The challenge for today is to love the unloved.

Pray that God will show you who you can reach out to today. Wherever you walk, have the mind-set of Jesus. Reach out to the homosexual, to the kid with the zits who has no friends, to the foul-mouth kid who is full of hate toward others (toward peers and teachers), or to the shy kid sitting alone at lunch. Maybe start with a "hello" and work up to a time you can sit with them. Start with a little gift or card or cookies. You can't go wrong with cookies! Do something as a group with others Christians. Let this person feel the love of many and not just one. You and your friends can all sit with this person at lunch.

A group of students stood outside every morning before school playing hacky sack. They were a rough-looking crowd and not so popular. A few of our youth bought four new hacky sacks with a Jesus sign on them. They gave the students the hacky sacks along with a hand-written card, expressing Jesus' love for them, and two dozen homemade cookies. They loved it! They were so appreciative. Did they get saved? No, but a seed of Jesus' love was planted in their hearts. The leader of the group did admit he should be going to church. We'll keep loving them and trust God to bring the change.

I pray it goes well!

LOL

Testimony or Comments:

Day 26
Invite to Church

Friday

Read Matthew 22:1–14.

HAVE YOU EVER BEEN INVITED to a wedding or wedding reception and just dreaded going? Maybe you didn't like the
bride or maybe even the groom. Perhaps the one side of
the family had the reputation of being drunks and you dreaded
being at the reception for fear of the scene that someone would
make. I remember being at a reception and my drunk relative
(my dad's age) was being disrespectful to some of the women
there. It was embarrassing, and I was not happy. The passage
you just read is talking about a wedding banquet you *don't* want
to miss.

Matthew 22:1–14 is a parable that talks about all those who
are married to Christ—in other words, all those who have a
relationship with Jesus. The wedding banquet mentioned in
this passage is a wonderful celebration that will take place in
heaven. The final banquet we could ever attend will be the one
in heaven with the Lord. This banquet will last forever and is
only for the followers of Christ. It is only for those who accept
His invitation. However, there will be *many* who will not accept
His invitation and will spend eternity in the lake of fire called

hell, *"where there will be weeping and gnashing of teeth."* There will even be those who will think they deserve heaven because they feel they were "good enough." However, because they never had a relationship with Jesus—the groom—they will not be allowed in. Let's look at this passage.

Verses 1–3 of this parable mention the wedding banquet, which is heaven. The king is God and the son is Jesus. The servants are the prophets of the Old Testament. You see, ever since the book of Genesis, God had the plan of sending Jesus into the world to save sinners. Our sin problem has separated us from God. Because of God's great love for us, He made a plan to one day send His Son, Jesus, to take our punishment. This way our sins could be forgiven and we could spend eternity with Him in heaven. In fact, God (the king) sent His prophets (the servants) to tell everyone about the coming of Jesus and the banquet. As you read throughout the Old Testament, you'll see where several of the prophets were either beaten or killed because the people did not want to listen to anything the prophets said. The people, including the so-called religious leaders, did not want to change their sinful ways and surrender their lives to the Lord.

Look how persistent God is in verse 4. God is so in love with His creation, and wants so much for everyone to attend His banquet, that He keeps inviting the people. Unfortunately, you see in verses 5 and 6 how the people made several excuses why they did not want a part of Jesus. Some even killed those who announced this big event. Those who reject Jesus will not have a part of heaven. But look again at God's persistence in verses 9–10. He went to those who we feel would never have responded to Christ's invitation. He went to the streets and gathered the good and the bad, and these people responded to God's invitation and were willing to turn to Christ. As a result, they got to be a part of the wedding banquet—heaven. In verses 11–13 we see a man standing before God because he felt he was "good enough" to get into heaven. But our good deeds are not what save us; it is a relationship with Christ. So many people put so much emphasis on being "good enough" and forget that we are all sinners and we all need the forgiveness of Jesus. Just as the man in this passage did not get to benefit heaven without a relationship with Jesus, neither will any of us.

Let me ask you a question. Do you have a relationship with Jesus? Have you accepted His forgiveness for your sins and are you living for Him? If not, you can do that right now. You can stop and pray this prayer: *"Dear Jesus, I am a sinner separated from God forever. I need forgiveness. Jesus, You paid the penalty for my sin, so right now I ask for Your forgiveness, I accept Your forgiveness and I thank You for that forgiveness. Please send me Your Holy Spirit and help me to grow in my faith in You. I surrender my life to You so I can live the life You have called me to. In Jesus' name, amen!"*

If you prayed this prayer for the first time, then let me congratulate you. Also, let me know or let a Christian leader know so we can help you get grounded in the Word of God and in Christian fellowship.

Now what about your friends? You know which ones I'm talking about. Remember the names of those who you mentioned in a previous challenge, those who were lost without Christ? Would you like to see them experience the same gift you have so they can be a part of the same wedding banquet one day? It's either heaven or hell. There is no place in between. People need a relationship with Jesus.

Here is your challenge: Think of one of your friends who doesn't have a relationship with Jesus and invite them to a Christian event.

Whether you are a teen or an adult, you could invite them to church this Sunday morning and/or Sunday school. You could invite them to the Sunday night gathering. If you invite them and they are hesitant to attend a gathering within a church building, then plan on inviting them to an event the church is doing outside of the church. Churches have special events for both youth and adults. This is an opportunity to get them exposed to Christian fellowship in hopes of hearing the truth about Jesus or seeing that Christians are more "cool" than they thought. Remember, going to church is not what saves you, but the goal is to expose them to an atmosphere that reflects Christ in hopes that they would want to give their lives to Jesus. Be prepared to answer any questions they may ask you. Lovingly ask them to attend, and if they decline, you could lovingly be persistent; and if they decline again, then respect their decision. Tell them you respect their decision and then keep praying for them. God will give you other opportunities to invite them again. Trust the Holy Spirit to lead you and give you the right heart in talking and responding to them. The biggest testimony they may see about Jesus may not be the church—it may be your life. So stay faithful to the Lord; that could be what helps them come to Christ and church at a later time.

Testimony or Comments:

Day 27 *Saturday*

"Come On, Be Nice"

COME ON, BE NICE!*"* Have you ever heard those words before? I have. Unfortunately, I heard it as a young kid from my parents, my grandparents and my friends; and I think I may have even heard it from my wife once. If I want to be really honest, I probably should have heard it more often than I did. I'm from a family of six: my mom and dad (of course), my two brothers and one sister. One morning my dad, my two brothers and I were at the breakfast table eating. My mom was in the kitchen fixing us some French toast. For whatever reason, we were calling for our dog. As we were calling for our dog, guess who came down the stairs and stepped into our presence? Yes, my sister. Well, we thought that was pretty funny! We were calling for the dog and our sister shows up. And from that time on, "dog" became our sister's nickname.

We would call our sister "dog" when we were trying to be funny or make fun of her, or when we wanted to hurt her or just plain be mean (not nice). When do you find yourself most wanting to be "not nice"? When you want someone to feel bad so you look good? When someone wrongs you? When they show you disrespect? When you want to get even? When you are asked to do something or, worse yet, you are told to do something? How dare someone tell us to do something! They should be nice about it. Right? Isn't that how we think? We will be nice when they are nice to us first! Unfortunately, that is not at all how Jesus did it, nor is it how He is asking us to do it. Why?

Jesus says to be nice first because our being nice is actually what changes the hearts and attitudes of others. We want the other person to change, and we think that if we act like them and not be nice, then they will change. But that is not how it works. In fact, when we are nice to others, it begins to even change our hearts and attitudes toward others. Not being nice either maintains the hate feelings between you and others or keeps the hate feelings within yourself.

What we don't realize is that our kindness is what actually helps build relationships and not tear them down. If we could just swallow our pride and quit thinking that people have to "earn" our love or kindness, what a better world this would be.

Read Proverbs 11:16–17; 12:25; 14:21, 31; and Matthew 5:38–42.

This may look like a lot of reading, but it isn't. Let's look at each passage you read. Proverbs is a great book to gain wisdom for our everyday living.

Proverbs 11:16 says a kind person gains the respect of others. But a ruthless person will not gain respect. They may become rich because of their selfishness and not caring for others, but they will never gain the respect of others.

Proverbs 11:17 states that a kind person will benefit themselves. We *benefit* when we are *nice*. But it also states that a cruel and not-so-nice person only brings trouble on themselves. Perhaps we can look back and think of times when we got in trouble and pinpoint where it all started—when we were not being nice.

Proverbs 12:25 says our kind words can help cheer another person up. We all need that, don't we? We all have days when we are anxious about something and need someone to come along and cheer us up with some nice words.

Proverbs 14:21 stresses the importance of being kind to the needy. Imagine how we can bless someone by helping meet one of their needs. Perhaps they are in need of a coat or in need of a friend to sit with at lunch. There are needs all around us, and God could use us to help meet them. In fact, **Proverbs 14:31** says being kind to the needy honors God.

Too often we want to return evil for evil done to us. Let's focus on being nice and meeting needs or saying kind words. **Matthew 5:38–42** says we must not return an "eye for an eye" or "tooth for a tooth." This means don't get revenge. In the Old Testament, if a person got his tooth knocked out by someone, then he would knock their tooth out. Jesus is saying in this Matthew passage, "Don't get revenge!" It never brings closeness in a relationship. Instead, be nice back to them.

 Your challenge today is to be nice to as many people as possible.

In fact, set a goal of 12 people. This could be fun. Imagine how many people you could impact today. But do it expecting nothing in return. Do it just because you are asked to do it. Trust the Holy Spirit to work in the other person's heart and in your heart as well. Be nice to some of your friends who don't know

Jesus. Be nice to your family members, to your teachers, to your enemies, to your classmates who sit next to you in school, to your coworkers, to your neighbors, to the person who waits on you at McDonald's, to the gas attendant, to whoever God puts in front of you.

During the time I wrote this devotional, God has given me three opportunities to be nice. I went out and started three vehicles for my wife and two daughters and scraped off the ice from their windows. God will give you opportunities. You just need to be willing to let Him use you.

Your acts of kindness could be speaking kind words; helping someone with their lunch; meeting another type of need; sending a nice encouraging card, letter or bouquet of flowers; or giving compliments. A quick compliment of a few words could change the hearts and attitudes of many people. Pick up something someone drops on the floor, run an errand, clean the house for your parents, or just do your chores without being asked—the list of countless ways of being nice to others goes on. God will give you the chances; be ready when it happens. At the end of the day, write down the names of 12 people you blessed today with your being nice.

Testimony or Comments:

Day 28 *Sunday*

"Watch Your Mouth"

YOU HAVE A BIG NOSE!" Unfortunately I've heard that comment more than once. What are our insecurities? Why do they become our insecurities? At the age of eight years old, my twin brother and I were at the skating rink. It was a popular spot that my whole family enjoyed as we were growing up. One particular day at the rink, we were having a fun time. I say "fun" because my brother and I were being chased by girls on skates. Now, at this age you act like you don't want girls chasing you, but deep down inside you love the attention. It makes you feel good. At times we would escape the girls' pursuit by entering the snack bar. I remember being at one end of the snack bar while this one girl stood at the opposite end. She was chasing me, but at this moment we both stared at each other, trying to determine our next move. We were smiling when all at once she made a random comment. She said, "Do you know the difference between you and your brother?" With a smile, I said, "What?" She replied "You have a BIG nose!" That hurt! I lost my smile very quickly. From that time on I became self-conscious of my "big" nose, and it became a point of insecurity.

116

The sad thing is this sort of thing has happened to *all* of us. When we look in the mirror, there is something we don't like about ourselves, and oftentimes it's because of what somebody else has said. I can tell horror stories of mean and rude comments people have said. Here's one example: A junior high boy was walking home from school. He was smiling and walked past three girls who were together. As he passed by, one girl made fun of his "buck" teeth. Then the three girls started laughing. His smile also left immediately. I can also tell stories of things people said very innocently but that were taken by the recipients as mean comments. A girl in ninth grade secretly "loved" a boy in school. Her mind was often filled with thoughts of him. She had him as a partner in art class one day, and she was so excited. The teacher had them stand in a light so their shadow was projected on a large piece of paper. Their partner then traced their shadow on the large paper with a marker. When the "cute" boy completed the drawing, he innocently said to the girl, "Wow, I never realized how disproportionate your head was to your body." Whoa! This comment destroyed her. She interpreted the comment as "You are fat!" This resulted in a four-year battle with an eating disorder.

I can go on with stories of people who have wanted to commit suicide because they heard negative comments so much that they felt unloved, unaccepted, unappreciated and worthless. I'm sure you know people like that as well, and perhaps you may be one of them.

Read James 3:1–12 and Acts 4:32–37.

In James 3 we are introduced to the topic of the mouth (or the tongue). It's a very small part of our body, yet it can do such great damage. **James 3:9–10** makes a great observation about our mouths: *"With the tongue we praise our Lord and Father, and with it we curse men, who have been made in God's likeness. Out of the same mouth come praise and cursing. My brothers, this should not be."*

No matter what, it seems we can't keep our mouths under control, and we end up saying things we shouldn't. But how hard do we work at saying more encouraging comments instead of more hurtful comments? If people were to give us a nickname that described how encouraging we were, what name would they give us? Would it be "The Destroyer"? "The Blesser"? "The Crusher"? Or "The Quicker Picker-Upper"?

In **Acts 4:32–37** we read about how the Christians all came together and helped and shared with each other in big ways. One of the individuals who helped out is mentioned by name. In verse 36, it says that Joseph sold one of the fields he owned and took the money and gave it to the apostles so the money could be used to help other Christians in need. Although his name was Joseph, everybody referred to him by his nickname. His nickname was Barnabas, which means "Son of Encouragement."

 Today's challenge is to be a Barnabas to those around you. Today is Barnabas day!

From the time you get out of bed to the time you go back to bed later on, I want you to be an encouragement to those you come in contact with. Encourage people at home, people in church, those you socialize with afterward or those you converse with on your cell phone or regular phone. Whoever you are with, please be an encourager to them. Here are some suggestions of things you could do:

1. **Compliment** people that you see today. Compliment them on their appearance. Compliment them on their dress attire. Compliment them on their performance on a particular task. Any kind word you say will truly make a person's day. They will feel good and will appreciate you.

2. **Help someone** if they are doing a certain task today. They may need help carrying something, setting up tables or chairs, fixing something, etc. Help them and then compli-

ment them on their servant's heart, their hard work or even on the things mentioned in number one.

3. **Write a note** and give it to someone, expressing why you appreciate them so much. Sure you could text them, but a note or card is something they could keep and refer to as often as they like. A teacher gave a note with a compliment to one of her students. He appreciated the note so much he kept it with him. When the boy went into the military, he was shot and killed. But in his shirt pocket, they found the note the teacher had given him when he was in school. It meant that much to him.

4. **Give a gift** to someone showing your appreciation. The gift could also be something that helps them out with a need. It could even be a monetary gift (money).

Any of these things you do will make someone feel good, appreciated and loved. You could build someone's self-confidence, which could alter their life completely. You just can't imagine how impactful your words or actions truly are. They build up a life and sometimes even save a life. So be a great Barnabas today!

Testimony or Comments:

Day 29 *Monday*

I Was HUNGRY

A
S AN INTRODUCTION to Days 29 through 34, we will be focusing on **Matthew 25:31–46**, which talks about specific needs we should be meeting as Christians. People in need are the *hungry*, the *thirsty*, the *strangers*, those *lacking clothes*, the *sick* and the *prisoners*. What inspired me to want to devote my time to this? This passage was one of my favorite Bible passages way back in the early 1980s. I memorized this passage because it puts emphasis on putting faith into practice. For those of you who have gone through the book *40-Day Revolution* by Richard Mull, you know he devoted six days to this very passage. I would like to do the same thing because I have strong convictions about this passage.*

So let's read **Matthew 25:31–46.** If this was the only passage you ever read from the Bible, you could easily conclude that salvation is based on *works* alone and not on *faith*. This passage must be read within the context of the rest of the Bible, and the Bible declares that salvation is based on God's grace, our faith

---

*Richard Mull, *40-Day Revolution: A Strategy to Impact Your World for Christ. Student Edition* (Colorado Springs: NavPress, 2002).)

and not works. However, our works are to be evidence to others that we have faith.

Read Ephesians 2:1–10.

This passage deals directly with our sin conflict. It states that we once were dead in our sins, ready to face God's wrath—eternal punishment in hell. But because of God's great love for us and because of His being rich in mercy, He provided a way so we would not have to face His wrath. In verse 5 we see that God's love, mercy and grace are what drove Him to take care of our sin problem. Through the work of His Son, Jesus Christ, we are no longer dead in our sins but made alive with Christ. Christ took God's punishment, or wrath, on Himself in our place. He did so at the cross. He provided forgiveness of sins so we too will one day be raised up together with Christ and spend eternity in heaven with God the Father and His Son, Jesus.

Ephesians 2:8 sums up what was just said in verses 1–7. Because of God's grace and our faith in Christ Jesus for what He did for us, we can be saved. Verse 9 is a quick reminder that our good "works" are not what saves us. No one will ever be able to boast or brag before God that they deserve heaven because they were such "good" people! Once we understand this truth, we can move forward to better understand verse 10. As people of *faith*, we have a responsibility that ends up demonstrating our faith. God created us "in Christ Jesus to do good works." In fact, God prepared those of us with faith well in advance to be people who would live out their faith by doing good works. You see, *good works* don't save us; our *faith* does. But *if* we are people of faith, then the world will see our faith through our good works.

This is the context in which we must read **Matthew 25:31–46**. If we are people who have put our faith into Christ, then we will be people who will put our faith into practice. We will let God use us by meeting the needs of those around us. In fact, when we reach out to those in need around us, we will treat each person as if they are Jesus, because whatever we do or don't do for others, we are really doing or not doing for the Lord Himself. Having this mind-set will drive us and motivate us to be more willing to reach out to others and make sacrifices for others.

 The first challenge in Matthew 25:31–46 is meeting the need of those who are hungry.

Jesus said, *"I was hungry and you gave me something to eat."* Our challenge today is to feed the hungry. Here are some ideas you can do for an individual or needy family:

1. Buy a gift certificate from a grocery store or a restaurant and give it to a person in need.

2. Make a meal and give it to someone in need.

3. Take a particular person or family out for a meal. Not only are you feeding them, but you are also connecting with them as a friend.

4. If you know where a homeless person spends their time, take him or her a warm meal or treat him or her to a meal.

5. Donate nonperishable food (from your house and/or purchased from the grocery store) to a local food pantry or some other famine-relief program.

6. For school students, you could purchase one or more $5 gift cards from a fast-food restaurant and give them away at school to students who would appreciate them. You could put each gift card in an envelope with a card stating you want to show the love of God in a practical way today.

The two ideas below were inspired by Richard Mull's book *40-Day Revolution*. They are not quotes from his book, but they are inspired ideas.

1. You could "fast" your lunch at work or school and use the money instead to feed another coworker or student.

2. You could take a certain dollar amount ($10 or $20) and randomly pick a few individuals and then pay for their meal.

Realize that as you do these things, people will ask why you are doing them. Say something that points them to Christ. For example, you could say you wanted to show God's love in a practical way. You probably don't want to say, "You are a hungry person so I want to feed you!" It will make them feel embarrassed, inferior and not very valuable.

Testimony or Comments:

_____

_____

_____

_____

_____

_____

_____

_____

Day 30

Tuesday

I Was THIRSTY

REREAD Matthew 25:31–46 AND think about doing these things for someone and treating them as if they were Jesus Himself. Then read **John 4:1–42.**

In **John 4:1–3** Jesus was traveling from Judea to Galilee, and in doing so, He had to travel through Samaria. If you lived in Samaria, then you were a Samaritan, and Samaritans were neither Jews nor Gentiles (non-Jewish people). Actually they were a mixed breed of both. They were considered "half-breeds." They were hated by the Jews, and no Jew would associate with them—except one!

Jesus came into Samaria and stopped in the town of Sychar because He was both tired and thirsty. He stopped by Jacob's well around noontime, and a woman came to draw water. This was unusual, because typically women drew water in the morning so they were not carrying the water in the heat of the day. This particular Samaritan woman came at noon because her reputation was not positive among the people. They knew what kind of lifestyle she lived.

As she stopped at the well, Jesus asked her to draw Him some water. Wow! The fact that He spoke to her amazed the woman, because Jews don't associate with Samaritans. Even more amazing was that Jesus knew about her lifestyle and still chose to speak to her. Jesus was the thirsty person and wanted a drink, but He was looking at the Samaritan woman and knew she was *really* the thirsty person. He recognized her need for spiritual water. She had been seeking love and acceptance in relationships, and Jesus wanted to step into her life and give her Himself. Jesus wanted to meet the woman's spiritual need, and it all started with Jesus being thirsty and in need of water.

Jesus started the discussion with the physical water, which led into talking about Himself as a person who could provide her with water that would enable her to never thirst again. Now He had her attention, because she would want nothing more than to have this water so she wouldn't have to go to the well again to draw water. At this time Jesus asked her to bring her husband, which resulted in Him exposing her sin. Jesus didn't expose her sin like we do to people. He was not condemning. He didn't belittle her. He exposed her sin in a way that allowed Him to maintain her respect and attention.

Then it happened! The woman realized that Jesus was a "spiritual" man (a prophet) and started asking spiritual questions. She was no dummy. She knew that one day the Messiah was coming to the earth. Imagine how "blown back" she must have been when Jesus told her that *He* was the Messiah. She realized that she had been speaking to the Messiah, the Savior of the world. She went back to her town and told everyone about her encounter with Jesus the Messiah, and that resulted in many of the people getting saved over a period of two days. Isn't that what it's really all about? We are asked to meet the needs of those around us, but in the back of our minds we have to be thinking not just of the physical needs but also of the spiritual need of the people we encounter.

Jesus emphasized this with His conversation with His disciples after the woman left to her hometown. Look at the dialogue Jesus had with them in verses 31–38. They were concerned about Jesus' physical body, and Jesus again turned the discussion around and focused on what is really important—one's spiritual condition. There is a harvest of souls out there waiting for someone to be a part of. The Lord wants us to do His will by doing His work of reaching lost souls for eternal life.

The second challenge in Matthew 25:31–46 is meeting the need of those who are thirsty.

Jesus said, *"I was thirsty and you gave me something to drink."* Our challenge today is twofold.

1. Give someone something to drink.

2. Somehow communicate to them that Jesus can satisfy their spiritual thirst.

Here are some examples. Once again, I want to incorporate the ideas that inspired me from Richard Mull's book *40-Day Revolution*. They are not quotes from his book, but they are inspired ideas.

1. Buy a bunch of drinks. You could get 48 bottles of water pretty cheap. Perhaps you prefer getting some Gatorade or lemonade. But then give them away to people during lunch at school, at work or in your neighborhood. Give them to people outside your church if you have traffic of people going by.

2. Depending on the weather, you could get a thermos with a cold or hot drink and pass out cups of your drink.

3. Perhaps you could get a friend or several others to help you with this. You could have a little card tied to the drink with these two Bible verses written inside: *"Jesus answered,*

'Everyone who drinks this water will be thirsty again, but whoever drinks the water I give him will never thirst. Indeed, the water I give him will become in him a spring of water welling up to eternal life' " (**John 4:13–14**). On the little card you could also identify your local church and your ministry or youth group name with an address and phone number.

4. As you pass out the drinks, you could also say, "I hope this will satisfy your thirsty body, just as Jesus has satisfied my thirsty soul."

What you say or what is written on the card could realistically open up a discussion which could result in one or several people getting saved. You never know. Who would have ever thought that a woman looking for love in all the wrong places would have ended up being an evangelist in her hometown?

Testimony or Comments:

_____

_____

_____

_____

_____

_____

_____

_____

Day 31 *Wednesday*

I Was a STRANGER

AVE YOU EVER SAT in a room full of people but felt all alone? You were surrounded by people but yet you were by yourself. When I was a child getting ready to enter third grade, I was excited about the first day of school! You know how it is. You and your mom go shopping and buy all the new items you need: pencils, erasers, ruler, pencil/eraser bag, notebooks, binders and even a new lunch box. The excitement builds as you get closer. You even go shopping for new clothes. As you get home, you go through your clothes; and the night before school you have already laid out your favorite ones. You can't wait to "show off" all your new "cool" stuff. Do you remember the excitement of seeing everyone again? Don't we all want to feel connected to someone? If the truth be known, we all want to feel connected to a few people our age. I remember entering the classroom and seeing my friends and sitting near my closest ones. I remember the connection I felt with them.

Then it happened! Bonnie entered our classroom. You all know Bonnie. She is the one with the reputation of being very smart. As she entered, I am certain she had all the same experiences as the rest of us had. She had gone shopping with her mom and purchased a bunch of "cool" stuff and some awesome looking clothes. I am sure she shared the same excitement of coming to school and seeing everyone again and connecting again with the others. But as Bonnie entered the room, some student started to "boo" Bonnie, which resulted in the whole classroom "booing" her. Her smile of excitement and anticipation immediately turned into sadness, and her eyes watered with tears. Bonnie sat in a room full of people and felt all alone that day. I am certain she will remember that "nightmare" for the rest of her life.

How about people you know? As you look around the room at work or school, or as you walk down the hallway or sit in the lunchroom, can't you identify those who seem to be on the outside? They are the strangers who walk or sit by themselves. They don't feel connected with anyone. Maybe they are the "new" person or the one that looks different than others, or has older clothes, or smells "dirty." Perhaps they are a little rough or annoying. Regardless of who they are, I can guarantee you this: they all share the same needs as the rest of us. They want to be shown love and respect. Some of these people wear masks or have a hard wall of protection that does not let anyone in. The only way to get in is to break it down with small steps of love.

Matthew 25:35 is the verse that says, "*I was a stranger and you invited me in.*" Jesus said He was a stranger and we invited Him in. To invite someone in requires reaching outward to those who are unconnected to the world and bringing them into our world so that they do feel connected. Some may read this and say that while it sounds easy, to actually put it into practice is very difficult. There are risks! To welcome the stranger means possibly being labeled just like they are. It may mean losing some of your friends. You may be laughed at or ridiculed.

Jesus knows how it feels to be alone. He especially related to this when the crowd yelled, "Crucify Him!" Those who did yell under their breath to let Jesus go were definitely the minority.

To stick up for the stranger or reach outward to them means you will be the minority, but right and wrong is not determined by how many people decide to do it. Jesus invested His time in the outcasts and touched many lives. He asks us to do the same.

Read **Hebrews 13:1–2** and **Zechariah 7:8–14.** God's message is to welcome, love and accept strangers. He knows how Bonnie felt when she entered the room and people booed her. We all can probably relate in some way. We don't want to feel that way, and we should be willing to do whatever it takes and make whatever necessary sacrifices so that others don't feel the same. In Zechariah we read how important this was to the Lord. He said, *"Administer true justice; show mercy and compassion to one another."* He also said, *"Do not oppress . . . the alien or the poor."* He didn't stop there. He also said He would not listen to people who want something from Him when they do not listen to Him or obey Him.

Please let our hearts be broken for the strangers so that we treat them in the way God wants us to. Let us treat them as if they are Jesus Himself.

Our challenge today is to reach outward to the strangers who feel disconnected and welcome them into our world so that they feel connected.

Here are some suggestions. Think of those you know in your everyday routines. It could be those in your school, your job place, in your neighborhood, or perhaps in your church. Some of the ideas were inspired by Richard Mull's book *40-Day Revolution.* They are not quotes from his book, but they are inspired ideas.

1. If you see a new person at church, you could reach out and say hello or, better yet, forfeit sitting in the pew you *always* sit in and sit with them instead. A new person at

church is more apt to return if they feel connected with someone when they do attend. I see so many new people (youth and adults) quit coming or never returning because they don't feel connected when they do come.

2. Get one or more of your friends, if possible, and go and sit with the stranger at the lunch table. You may end up having to do it yourself, but you don't realize how much of a blessing you become when you do this. There are so many testimonies of people who have contemplated suicide but changed their minds when someone reached out to them.

3. If you are really nervous about doing this, then start this connecting process by saying hello when you walk by strangers or see them. Ask how they are doing. Make eye contact. What you will find is you make them more comfortable with you and you make it easier to reach out more in the future.

4. Perhaps on your way to school or work you could offer them a ride.

5. You could plan a fun night (bowling, board games, sledding, etc.) and invite that person and tell them to invite another person as well. That way they may feel more comfortable to come. Hopefully when they leave they will feel they gained some new friends.

6. Perhaps in your neighborhood there are people you don't know well or who rarely get visitors. Take a small gift over or some dessert or just yourself, and begin a bonding process with them. Tell them you were thinking of them and wanted to do something special. One student from our youth group occasionally visits one of her lonely neighbors. It started with cookies, but the last time she was there she visited for two hours. I can't explain how much that has meant to this neighbor.

Be a *blessing* to someone today!

DAY 31

Testimony or Comments:

_____

_____

_____

_____

_____

_____

_____

_____

_____

_____

_____

_____

_____

_____

_____

_____

_____

_____

Day 32

Thursday

I Needed CLOTHES

IT WAS A COLD WINTER day, but it wasn't snowing. I was on my way to see my girlfriend. I was in college but home on break. Who would have ever thought I would meet and date a girl in college whose hometown was less than 20 minutes from mine? What was great was that she loved Jesus and I loved Jesus. Prayer and Bible time were important to both of us. Sharing Jesus with others was also important to us.

On my way to pick her up I saw a gentleman hitchhiking. Now let me say this, as a young and naive college student, I often picked up hitchhikers. I don't recommend this, because of the dangers associated with it, but on this particular cold day I felt the desire to stop and give him a ride. The man did not have a winter coat. Instead he had a throw rug around his shoulders which did not completely cover his upper body. I drove by the man and pulled off the side of the road. I said a quick prayer to the Lord: "Father, please help me share Jesus with this man." I had WCTL Christian radio playing. I made sure the sound was just the right volume and waited for the opportunity.

The man looked cold, tired and exhausted and was smoking a long, thin cigar. I introduced myself and began a conversation

with him. I was excited to share Jesus with this man but struggled finding an opportunity because he was so unresponsive. I
mean, he answered my questions, but with short answers. He
was not very engaging. I asked his name, where he was from
and where he was headed. He was from New York; we were in
northern Pennsylvania. He was headed to Virginia. Other than
that, I struggled with how to share Jesus.

Finally, an open door of opportunity came to me. A song that
I liked came on the radio, and I asked the man if he had ever
heard of this singer on the radio. He said no, with great ex-
haustion and tiredness. I started to share how the singer loved
the Lord and sang great songs about Jesus. His response was,
"That's nice." I could see his tired eyes as he responded and felt
I was failing at my witnessing attempts. The ride seemed very
quick, as I reached the road where I had to turn. I apologized
that I wasn't going farther and pulled off the side of the road
so he could get out. Again, I was bummed because I felt that I
failed at my attempts to share Jesus with this man.

Just as the man was getting out of the car with his throw rug as
his coat, God spoke to me in my heart and mind. It wasn't an
audible voice but a very strong thought that entered my mind,
and I knew it was from God. He said to me, "Give the man
your coat!" *What?* What is God talking about? This is *my* coat!
My letter jacket from high school! It had pins and patches on
it from all my "wonderful" accomplishments in track and cross-
country. Surely God, you don't want me to give him *this* coat?
But as the man stepped out of the car, I quickly said to him,
"Sir, do you want my coat?" However, racing in my mind were
the words "Please say no, please say no, please say no!" His tired
response was, "No." A little guilt came over me when he answered no, so I asked him again: "Are you sure? You have a long
ways to go." Still racing in my mind were the words "Please say
no, please say no, please say no!" His tired response this time

was "No, that's okay, I'll get one when I get to Virginia." My response was "Okay!" He shut the door and I drove off.

What's sad about this story is I prayed for God to help me share Jesus with this man, but when God answered my prayer by telling me to give the man my coat, I was not obedient. I was unwilling to make the necessary sacrifice. What is sadder yet is that God never said, "Ask the man if he wants the coat!" but rather, "Give the man your coat!" Think of the witness and testimony that could have been for Jesus. This is what could have happened: The man gets out of the car and I get out, take off my coat, walk to his side of the car and say, "Here, Jesus wants you to have this coat." The dialogue that could have come from that could have been exciting.

In **Matthew 25:36a** and **40,** Jesus says, " *I needed clothes and you clothed me,* " a**nd** *"whatever you did for one of the least of these brothers of mine, you did for me."*

Your challenge today is to help Jesus by helping those who need clothes.

As you think of this challenge, realize it may mean making a sacrifice. Don't just go and find the old clothes with holes in them and give them to someone thinking you are being a huge blessing. A teacher once told me that if I, as a 15-year-old, did not want to wear my old worn-out shirts anymore because of my peers making fun of them, then why give them to some other 15-year-old and set them up to be made fun of? Why not be more sacrificial and give them some of your nicer shirts, even some of your nicer shirts you are not wearing that often? Pray before you give, and ask God what He would have you give. Here are some suggestions. Some of the ideas were inspired by Richard Mull's book *40-Day Revolution.* They are not quotes from his book, but they are inspired ideas.

1. If you know of a particular person who needs clothes and your size matches theirs, then go through your closet and drawers and give them some of yours.

2. Perhaps your family can all go through their clothes and take some to a needy family or give them to a Christian organization that distributes clothes.

3. Perhaps you can plan a clothes drive in your church or youth group and collect several clothes all at once. Some churches around Christmastime get the sizes of children's and adults' clothes, coats and boots and post a sign on the bulletin board asking the church to make donations. Some give clothes, some buy clothes and some give money so the church can purchase the clothes needed.

4. I suggest you include a card with the clothes you give away to a family that mentions how you want to express the love of Jesus through the giving of the clothes. I believe this is important. Remember what Jesus said in **Matthew 4:4**: *"It is written, 'Man does not live on bread alone, but on every word that comes from the mouth of God.'"* Our giving helps meet someone's physical need, but let us not forget their spiritual need as well. Just a small mention of Jesus' love will point their heart toward the Lord.

5. Clothing drives can also be done at your school or neighborhood. Talk with your principal about doing this, and it could become an annual event. The only problem with this is they may not let you mention the name of Jesus, but perhaps they would let you do it for your church.

Thanks for being a blessing!

Testimony or Comments:

_____

_____

_____

_____

_____

_____

_____

_____

_____

_____

_____

_____

_____

_____

_____

_____

_____

Day 33

I Was SICK

Friday

AS MY DAD LAY ON his deathbed after fighting cancer for seven years, my family sat in the living room waiting because we knew at any time he was going to meet the Lord. As we sat there, I watched my mom and reflected on how she had been by my dad's side for seven years. My dad never complained of his chemo or of the pain. His body's immune system would break down, and he would become very sick with a cold and even shingles in the face. Just thinking about it makes me wonder how anyone could go through what he did and not be a constant "pain" to others. His favorite saying was, "I can always think of others who are worse off than I am!"

My mom took care of my dad. What she did serves as a great example of what is mentioned in **Matthew 25:36**: *"I was sick and you looked after me."* My mom didn't just visit my dad on occasion, nor did she just pray for him. She got right down into the heart of my dad's life and invested her life into my dad's. She rarely left my dad's side. It was like that right up until my dad took his last breath on the bed in the living room. Don't get me wrong, my mom visited my dad in the hospital and prayed for him often, but she also "looked after" my dad. She took care of his every need and gave up many selfish desires to ensure that my dad was okay and well taken care of.

Read **Luke 10:25–37.** This passage is about a man who took care of another man. Jesus was confronted by a man wanting to test Jesus. This man was a scholar in the study of the Law. The man asked Jesus, *"What must I do to inherit eternal life?"* Jesus answered the man by asking him, *"What is written in the Law?"* The man answered by quoting the two greatest commandments: Love God with all of who you are and love your neighbor as yourself. Jesus told the man, *"Do this, and you will live."* But the scholar didn't stop there. He asked Jesus, *"Who is my neighbor?"* Jesus' response was nothing short of amazing: He told the story of a man who was beaten by thieves, stripped of his clothes and left to die on the side of a road.

The first two men who approached the man's dying body were both religious leaders. They were men who you would have expected to stop and take care of this man. However, they made sure they never went near the man and stayed as far away as possible. For whatever reason, they did not want to be concerned with this matter. Perhaps they were afraid of what might happen to them, or maybe they were in a big hurry to get somewhere else, or maybe they were just too busy. The third man who came by was a Samaritan man. This is the interesting part, because a Samaritan and a Jew did *not* get along and hated each other. In fact Samaritans and Jews would not even speak to one another and often made sure they had nothing to do with each other. The Samaritan is the *last* person you would think who would have anything to do with this dying Jew.

Look at what this passage says the Samaritan did for this man.

1. **"He took pity on him."** Perhaps that is our problem at times. We don't feel sorry for others, especially those we don't like. That could be the person at school who mistreats us or even our in-laws who we don't get along with

because we agree very little on everyday matters.

2. **"He went to him."** It's one thing to feel sorry for a person or have compassion on their situation, but it's another thing to actually take some kind of action toward helping them. That's where many people fail. They just can't get past "feeling sorry for" someone and don't move on to the next step of action.

3. **He took care of his wounds with medicine and with bandages.** It seems as if he responded without giving any selfish thought. He was more than willing to use his own supplies for another man, even an enemy.

4. **"He put the man on his own donkey, took him to an inn and took care of him."** Wow, he certainly went all out for this Jewish man. I'm certain this Samaritan had other things he could have been doing that day. He could have dropped the man off at the inn and gone on with his own business, but he took care of him even after he reached the inn. Fear did not stop him, and his busy schedule did not stop him from doing all he did.

5. **He gave the inn owner some cash.** The Samaritan finally left after feeling confident that the man was okay, but to make sure, he left some money for the inn owner to ensure that the Jewish man was continually taken care of. He even promised he'd be back and was willing to pay for any added expenses. The Samarian made the ultimate sacrifice in order to help the Jewish man. He reached into his wallet and pulled out the cash. Ouch! I fear that many of us would not go to that degree, but this man did.

Knowing what my mother and this Samaritan did, I feel this is what Jesus meant when He said, *"I was sick and you looked after me."* Obviously we can't take care of every sick person in the world, but I feel that **1 Timothy 5:3–8** makes it clear that we are to take care of our family first. After that, I feel we need to be sensitive to the Holy Spirit about who He would have us minister to. Be ready and willing to help whoever God puts in your path. Just beware because it may even be your enemy.

Today's challenge is to somehow invest in the life of a sick person.

Some of the ideas were inspired by Richard Mull's book *40-Day Revolution.** They are not quotes from his book, but they are inspired ideas.

1. Pray earnestly for anyone you know who is sick. Prayer is powerful, and let us not leave out what God is very capable of doing as He intervenes in a person's life.

2. You could go to the hospital and spend time talking with a few of the patients and offer a prayer before you leave. If it is the Christmas season, you could even get a group of friends and go up and down the hallways singing Christmas carols. Some of our youth have given manicures and pedicures to the elderly. It definitely lifts a person's spirits when you invest your life into their life.

3. Perhaps God has blessed you with money and you know someone who is unable to pay for medical treatment that the insurance company would not cover. You could be a blessing by paying or helping pay this unfortunate expense. If they ask you why you are so willing to do this, tell them it's a way of showing God's love for others.

4. You may know of someone who is sick in their own home. A visit to their home may be appreciated. Again, offer a prayer before you leave. I've seen people who want very little to do with God be very open for prayer when sick. If they say no, then just let them know you will be praying for them.

*Richard Mull, *40-Day Revolution: A Strategy to Impact Your World for Christ. Student Edition* (Colorado Springs: NavPress, 2002).

5. A phone call may also be a good idea.

6. Taking the time to write and send a get-well card would also be appreciated. They'll be glad to know you are thinking of them and that you are praying for them as well.

7. If you are unaware of anyone who is sick, then contact your church. They almost always know of someone who is going through a rough time physically.

I pray you have an awesome day!

Testimony or Comments:

_____

_____

_____

_____

_____

_____

_____

_____

_____

_____

_____

Day 34

Saturday

I Was in PRISON

IN MATTHEW 25:36 JESUS SAYS, "*I was in prison and you came to visit me.*" You may have visited a prison before. If you haven't, you have seen television shows concerning prisons or those in prisons. You may have even seen a television show on the life of a prisoner. In fact, some who read this may have been in prison or have had a family member in prison at one time or another. What I have learned is that life in prison is no different than life outside the prison walls. You have Christians and non-Christians. You have those who attend church and those who don't. You have those who want to succeed and those who don't. You have those who want to impact people's lives for good and those who are all about themselves.

I remember visiting a prison near Washington, DC, a few times, and my visit was with a man who was a convicted murderer and was serving a life sentence. While in prison, he met the Lord and later wanted to somehow impact lives outside of the prison walls. His passion was for those with certain disabilities. He put together a program that reached out to youth with disabilities, and it was implemented by people on the outside who trusted what he formed as being from the Lord. After several years of being implemented within the surrounding communities, his program became very successful. It impacted the lives of many with disabilities and captured the attention of people within the community and across the United States. Our congress men and women were so amazed at this program that they gave a congressional award to the man in prison.

It all started with two men who went into the prison and asked the man how they could help meet his needs. Over a long period of time, the prisoner was so impacted by their love for him that he gave his life to the Lord. That's a great praise for the Lord! Unfortunately I have stories where I have invested time and money in a prisoner who became so close to the Lord while in prison but after being released walked away from his commitment to the Lord. These stories are sad and difficult to handle at times, but God wants us to be faithful and minister to those in prison regardless of the outcome.

I did an extensive study in the Bible regarding people in prison. I have found this to be a very, very popular topic. I also found that God is concerned about those who are in prison physically and spiritually. So even though you may not know anyone who is in prison physically, I am confident you know of people who are in prison spiritually. There are numerous Bible passages you could read for today, but I chose just a few. It may take extra time looking them up, but it will be worth it. Please read them in the order that they are written.

Read Isaiah 61:1, Luke 4:16–21, Acts 8:18–23, Revelation 1:4–6 and John 8:31–38

In **Isaiah 61:1** we read about a man who will one day come to this earth and will minister to the poor, the brokenhearted, those captive or in prison, the blind and the oppressed. In this passage, it doesn't say what this man's name will be, but God was talking about the coming day of Jesus. Hundreds of years after this passage was written, after Jesus did appear, He read this passage before the people in the synagogue. We read in **Luke 4** that after Jesus had read this Isaiah passage, He looked at His listeners and told them He is the One who God had sent. And, like people respond today, when Jesus told them He is the chosen One of God, a few believed and many did not.

In **Acts 8** we read that those who are living in sin are the ones who are held captive. The Good News, mentioned in **Revelation 1:4–6**, is that Jesus loves us and has freed us from our sins by shedding His blood. Those who don't know Jesus remain prisoners of their sins. Those who surrender their lives to Christ are set free from the penalty of sin and have a relationship with God through Christ. **John 8** says the truth of Christ will set us free, and when we are free we are "free indeed"—it is a matter of fact! This freedom is first and foremost for our spiritual need, but Christ also died for our physical needs along with our emotional and mental needs.

Those of us who have a love relationship with Jesus can share His love with others who are prisoners of their sin or prisoners in a prison cell.

The challenge is to touch someone's life that is in prison.

Some of the ideas were inspired by Richard Mull's book *40-Day Revolution.** They are not quotes from his book, but they are inspired ideas.

Students and adults: there should be an idea here that would work for you.

---

*Richard Mull, *40-Day Revolution: A Strategy to Impact Your World for Christ* . Student Edition. (Colorado Springs: NavPress, 2002).

1. Give a Christian book or magazine to a student in detention to read.

2. Actually work it out with the principal to take detention for someone else. In fact, work it out that the principal allows you to explain why the other student is not doing detention and why you are. You could tell them that you want them to get a picture of what Jesus did for us when He went to the cross and took our punishment.

3. Perhaps your pastor or youth pastor could set it up so that a group of you could visit a prison cell or someone in prison.

4. Two websites you could go to that offer suggestions are www.Christianpenpals.com and www.pfm.com. One of the ideas they suggest is writing to a prisoner. I would caution this without strict parental guidance. I did this once when I was younger, and the man I wrote to was more interested in what I could send him than my friendship. He wanted cigarettes and money.

5. Another idea is if you know someone who has served time in the prison system and is currently out, you could write them an encouraging letter. Let them know you are praying for them. Take over a meal or baked goods and spend some time with them. They usually need a lot of encouragement because it is easy to get recaught up in the world once they get out. Anything you do for them could be very helpful. I would encourage not meeting with someone of the opposite sex unless you have others who go with you.

6. You may know some who are prisoners of an addiction: drugs, alcohol, sex, bullying or something else. Perhaps you could reach out to them by asking what need they may have because you or your church would like to help them in some way. Whether it be taking up a collection

and putting it toward a need or doing something practical, like helping them cut wood, you'd be surprised at how it could change their heart and life.

Testimony or Comments:

_____

_____

_____

_____

_____

_____

_____

_____

_____

_____

_____

_____

_____

Day 35

Sunday

Pray for Others

READ JOHN 17:1–21 SLOWLY and carefully. As you read it, think about these two questions: (1) Who was Jesus praying for? (2) What was His concern?

In John 17:1–5 Jesus prayed for Himself because it was soon time for Him to go to the cross of redemption. Jesus was about to do the very thing that would give eternal life to all who would believe and follow Him. But interesting enough, His prayer for self was that God would be glorified.

In John 17:6–19 Jesus prayed for His disciples. While Jesus was on earth, God gave the disciples into His hands to minister to and teach and train. Jesus knew that when He would leave the earth, the disciples would have a challenge ahead of them in sharing the message of Jesus to others. Jesus wanted God to be glorified through them. He asked God to protect them and keep them unified in faith. He concluded His prayer for the disciples by asking that they be sanctified. Jesus wanted them to be holy and pure in the world they were going to minister to. He wanted them set apart so they would not live according to the worldly standards but by the standards of God so that other lives could be reached.

In John 17:20–21 Jesus prayed for all the future believers.
Let's answer the questions asked in the beginning. Who was
Jesus praying for? He prayed for Himself, the disciples and for
future believers in the Christian faith. What was His concern?
His concern was threefold: He wanted God to be glorified,
His followers to be protected and new Christians to be steady
in the faith.

Throughout Jesus' life, He was always concerned about others
and their needs. His concern drove Him to invest Himself in
their lives so their needs could be met, but the ultimate goal
was for their souls to be saved from sin and have new life in
Himself. He couldn't even pray without having concern for the
souls of others. He wanted God to be glorified.

When we pray for others, what are our motives? Is it just so
people will "feel" better, or is there a deeper concern? Are we
looking not just at their earthly needs but also at the needs of
their souls?

> **My challenge is that we will pray for
> others and be concerned about their
> earthly needs as well as their souls.**

Who should we pray for? Jesus prayed for both believers and
those who had not yet become believers. So pick one to five believers and one to five non-believers who you want to see come
to know Christ. Perhaps you could pick the names from your
"Unsaved List" you did in a previous challenge for the unsaved
people.

Write on a piece of paper the names of the people you are going to pray for, and then ask those people specifically what their
prayer concerns are. Say to the unsaved, "I put a list together
of my friends who I want to pray for regularly, but I'm not al-

ways sure what their needs are. Is there anything you are going through that I could be praying for you about?" Of course, you will be praying for their lost souls, but don't tell them you are praying that their lost souls will go to heaven instead of hell! Rather, focus on identifying their earthly needs, as Jesus did, and through your prayers God can use you, others or a miracle to meet their needs. This, in turn, can be used to point them to Christ.

But as you pray, do the following three things:

1. **Pray in faith, believing God will work; and do not doubt. James 1:6** states that when we ask God, we must ask in faith, believing, for those who ask with doubt will not receive anything.

2. **Pray with thanksgiving, believing God will work. Philippians 4:6** says, *"Do not be anxious about anything, but in everything, by prayer and petition, with thanksgiving, present your requests to God."* By saying "Thanks" in advance, you are saying, "God, I trust you!"

3. **Don't stop praying for them. Colossians 1:9** says we are not to stop praying for others. In other words, don't do this just once, but do it on an ongoing basis and periodically find out how they are doing. You'd be surprised how this communication will help believers be encouraged and help their minds to be focused on the Lord. For unbelievers, it could also help them gain interest in spiritual things, which gives you a chance to share your faith in Christ. Do you see how this can work wonders?

Now as you pray, realize God's answer may not be so they "feel" better. He may have them going through tough times as a way of getting them focused on Him. God's ultimate goal before physical healing is that He is glorified (like in Jesus' prayer) and that people's souls are in Christ. Lastly, He wants to conform us into the image of Christ. Keep that in mind.

Testimony or Comments:

_____

_____

_____

_____

_____

_____

_____

_____

_____

_____

_____

_____

_____

Day 36 *Monday*

Reminder of Love

HELP, I NEED SOME LOVE! Have you ever felt like you were drowning in a sea of loneliness or depression or isolation? Have you ever felt a lack of appreciation—even from God—and you just wanted to scream, "HELP, I NEED SOME LOVE!"

I remember a farmer telling a true story about something that happened to him. The farmer was milking cows in his barn. He was going through a rough time. That particular day was a difficult one for him, and he was feeling a little depressed. Sometimes when you are isolated from the world and surrounded by your work, you feel alone and unloved. That is how he was feeling when, all of a sudden, his little son come running down the middle of the barn toward him. As he was running, his arms were stretched outward, and he was yelling, "Daddy!" And when he reached his daddy, he leaped into his arms and wrapped his little arms around his dad's neck and said (with excitement), "I LOVE YOU!" As the farmer shared his story, he said that seeing, hearing and feeling his boy's love changed his whole emotional well-being! Seeing, hearing and feeling his son's love made him go from feeling down to being on cloud nine. It was a real "lifter-upper"!

When I heard that story, I couldn't help but feel that when our Father God sees us feeling down, He allows circumstances to happen in our lives as a reminder to us that He loves us, or that we are special, or that we are important, or that we are valuable. The farmer probably knew his son loved him that day, but God knew this farmer, in his conflicting moment, needed a little reminder of his value and worth. So God sent the little boy down and let him express to his daddy just what he needed to hear at that particular moment.

A young lady struggling with her marriage was feeling as if God was so far away. But as she read her Bible that morning, she was reminded by a passage she read that God was near to her and would never leave her. I don't remember the passage she read, but God knew she needed a reminder and provided one at a crucial moment.

Can you relate to any of these incidences? I think we can all relate in some way to a time when we needed a reminder of how loved we really are, or of how special, valuable or important we are. Perhaps there is someone in your life who needs that reminder.

Read Deuteronomy 31:8, Joshua 1:9, Psalms 138:1–8 and 139:1–18.

Please, as you read these passages, let God speak to your heart what you need to be reminded of today. These are verses God has provided for me in the past as a reminder of His love for me. They helped remind me that He is always with me so I don't have to be distressed and discouraged, that He always loves me despite my failures and that He is always faithful to me even when I am not faithful to Him. He always has a listening ear when I call on Him. Even though He is a BIG God, He looks upon me, a lowly person. When in trouble, He saves me. His love endures forever.

Psalm 139 is packed with reminders of how much God loves us and how valuable and important we are. I will just mention three of them: God's right hand holds us tight and close. He reminds us that we are wonderfully made. We are not mistakes. The precious thoughts God has for us are more numerous than the grains of sand. Wow!

The Scriptures are filled with countless reminders of God's love for us.

 My challenge is just as God reminds us of His love, remind someone today of your love for them.

Maybe someone you know is drowning in a sea of loneliness or depression or isolation, or feeling a lack of appreciation. Even though they don't show it on the outside, perhaps they are yelling on the inside, "HELP, I NEED SOME LOVE!" Who needs your love? Husbands, how about your wife? Wives, how about your husband? Perhaps your kids have been yelled at so much lately they need to be reminded of your love in a special way. Children, perhaps you have done little in listening to and obeying your parents' wishes or commands. They get so stressed out too! Trust me on this one: they would appreciate a reminder of your love. Flowers and a card could do wonders in bringing a tear of joy. Don't forget about your grandparent living at home alone, or your neighbor, or a close friend you have taken for granted, and the list goes on. Who would God have you reach out to with your love?

Suggestions: Put a banner up in the house saying "I Love You!" Or decorate someone's room with some streamers and a sign listing 12 things that you love about that person. Sure, you could do a card with cookies. Other options still exist. Get six of the person's closest friends to write on a card what they appreciate about the person you chose, and then give it to them. Maybe you could all write on a decorated poster board. Maybe a strong hug with the words "I love you" will suffice. Some people just like to be taken out of the house. My grandma appreciates being taken out for a meal. Some like an afternoon drive in the country or enjoy seeing Christmas lights and decorations in the city. Have fun!

Oh, yeah, just in case you forget—I LOVE YOU!

Testimony or Comments:

_____

_____

_____

_____

_____

_____

_____

_____

_____

Day 37

Tuesday

Isn't Learning Fun?

DURING THESE NEXT THREE DAYS (Days 37, 38 and 39), our focus is going to be on sharing our faith verbally in some way. Days 37 and 38 will be our preparation time. Day 39 will be the actual challenge of sharing our faith with someone. Until this point, most of our challenges have been on touching lives through acts of kindness followed by sometimes mentioning the love of Jesus in some manner. I'm a firm believer that as we love people, as we have done in the last 30 days, we connect with them in a way that builds respect between us and them. Once this happens, they are more receptive to what we have to say about Jesus when God gives us that chance to share. I realize these challenges will require more knowledge of God's salvation plan, more faith and trust in God to help us share our faith, and more strength from God to get us out of our comfort zones and build our confidence. Days 37 and 38 will help accomplish this.

Sharing the message of Jesus means we are sharing the gospel message. If someone asks if you know the "gospel message," they are talking about the salvation message of Jesus. So in helping you share the message of Jesus, we are going to use the word *gospel* as an acronym. I learned this when we attended the Dare 2 Share conference founded by Greg Stiers. (By the way, get on Greg's website and attend one of these conferences: www.dare2share.org. Our teens grew tremendously after attending. We go every year now). You can actually see in more detail what I am going to share with you by getting on his website: www.dare2share.org/gospeljourney.

Here is what I mean. The salvation message of Jesus can be summed up by using the acronym GOSPEL. Here is what each letter stands for:

G – **G**od loves us and created us to be with Him.
O – **O**ur sins separated us from God.
S – **S**ins cannot be removed by our good deeds.
P – **P**aying the price for sin, Jesus died and rose again.
E – **E**veryone who trusts in Jesus alone has eternal life.
L – **L**ife with Jesus means a changed life.

If you did get on Greg Stiers's Gospel Journey website, you'll notice I added "God loves us" to the letter G, and I use a different definition for the letter L. I do so because I want people to know the importance of a changed life after meeting Jesus. Greg emphasizes this truth, just not in the acronym. However, I do want it incorporated within the acronym.

Your challenge today is to memorize and learn what each letter stands for.

Go over it, over and over again. This is called repetition. Please take the time to do this. Learning this will literally save a person's life. Tomorrow's challenge will be learning to articulate it. You'll pretend you are actually sharing it with someone. However, today's challenge is to memorize the meanings. Set a goal of a minimum of 15 minutes to do this.

PHASE 1: First memorize the definition of each letter that is mentioned above. When completed, move to Phase 2.

PHASE 2: Now memorize the definitions along with the Scripture references mentioned below. I'm not asking you to memorize the verses right now, just the references (book of Bible, chapter and verses). Certainly become familiar with what each one says, and if you do memorize them, it will only be helpful later on. But for now you can just worry about where the verses are found.

G – God loves us and created us to be with Him. *"So God created man in his own image, in the image of God he created him; male and female he created them"* (**Genesis 1:27**).

O – Our sins separated us from God. *"There is not a righteous man on earth who does what is right and never sins"* (**Ecclesiastes 7:20**). *"For all have sinned and fall short of the glory of God"* (**Romans 3:23**).

S – Sins cannot be removed by our good deeds. *"For it is by grace you have been saved, through faith—and this is not from yourselves, it is the gift of God—not by works, so that no one can boast"* (**Ephesians 2:8–9**). So we are saved by God's grace and our faith in Jesus, not by our works; so we can never boast or brag how we are good enough to get into heaven. We need Jesus.

P – Paying the price for sin, Jesus died and rose again. *"In fact, the law requires that nearly everything be cleansed with blood, and without the shedding of blood there is no forgiveness . . . But now [Christ] has appeared once for all at the end of the ages to do away with sin by the sacrifice of himself"* (**Hebrews 9:22, 26b**).

E - Everyone who trusts in Jesus alone has eternal life. *"For*

God so loved the world that he gave his one and only Son, that whoever believes in him shall not perish but have eternal life" (**John 3:16**). *"Jesus answered, 'I am the way and the truth and the life. No one comes to the Father except through me' "* (**John 14:6**). *"Salvation is found in no one else, for there is no other name under heaven given to men by which we must be saved"* (**Acts 4:12**).

L – Life with Jesus means a changed life. *"If anyone is in Christ, he is a new creation; the old has gone, the new has come!"* (**2 Corinthians 5:17**). *"But you will receive power when the Holy Spirit comes on you; and you will be my witnesses in Jerusalem, and in all Judea and Samaria, and to the ends of the earth"* (**Acts 1:8**).

Don't let yourself be filled with high anxiety if you don't get this 100 percent. It takes time and commitment. You'll do just fine, but do commit to a minimum of 15 minutes for study.

Testimony or Comments:

_____

_____

_____

_____

_____

_____

_____

_____

Day 38 *Wednesday*

I Hate Studying

"I HATE STUDYING!" Have you ever said those words? "It's no fun!" Hey, you don't have to try and convince me. I don't like studying either. My worst memories of college life were when I pulled all-nighters so I could study for an exam. I could remember getting 8 hours sleep in a 72-hour period. That's three hours one night, three hours the next night and two hours the last night. But just because we don't like something doesn't mean it's not a good thing.

Read **Ezra 7:1–10**. Don't get bogged down with all the names. Focus on Ezra the priest and teacher. Ezra had asked King Artaxerxes, king of Persia, for items to take with him to Jerusalem. This passage says that the king granted Ezra everything he requested. Twice in this passage it says God's hand was on Ezra.

1. The first time it says the king gave Ezra everything he asked for because *"the hand of the Lord his God was on him."*

2. The second time it mentions that the hand of God was on Ezra, it states why: *"For Ezra had devoted himself to the study and observance of the Law of the Lord, and to teaching its decrees and laws in Israel."* Can you imagine this? The almighty hand of God—the Creator of the universe—had His hand on Ezra His creation. Why? Because Ezra was

committed or devoted to *studying* God's Word, *obeying* God's Word and *teaching* God's Word.

Think now of the impact we could have for the Lord in reaching lost souls if we were to be committed to studying, obeying and teaching or sharing God's Word. As we commit to these same three things, we will see the mighty hand of God not just on us but working through us. Your life will change and so will the lives of others for the glory of God!

Yesterday you studied what the acronym GOSPEL meant and became familiar with some of the Scripture verses.

> **Today's challenge is to practice articulating how you could present this GOSPEL in conversation.**

Practice this as if you are presenting the whole thing to an individual. While I was in the process of learning this, I got into a conversation with someone about the love of God. So I shared with this person about **G**—God's love. Another time I was in a conversation with someone about how Christians are to live. Then I jumped to the letter **L**. You see, as you study and learn this, God will use this information in more than one way in conversations with others. After you study this and practice presenting it, you'll find that when you get into a conversation with someone, you become increasingly more comfortable and confident. The nervous feelings, however, never go away, but it does get easier! You'll also find yourself presenting it differently each time, but with the same "heart message." That's good! But we have to start somewhere, so let's start with getting some kind of dialogue written down.

Either write on a piece of paper or type on your computer a dialogue of how you could share with someone. Commit to writing your dialogue no matter how long it takes. I'll do mine here as an example to help you. I have the acronym mentioned below so you can refer to it.

G – **G**od loves us and created us to be with Him.
O – **O**ur sins separated us from God.
S – **S**ins cannot be removed by our good deeds.
P – **P**aying the price for sin, Jesus died and rose again.
E - **E**veryone who trusts in Jesus alone has eternal life.
L – **L**ife with Jesus means a changed life.

Here we go! I'll write my dialogue as if I'm sharing with some-one who asked about heaven and hell. Before I'd share, I'd ask them what they believe. I'd let them share any crazy ideas they have and never stop them or "correct" them. When they fin-ished, I'd say:

Well, this is what I believe. I believe it all starts with God. The Bible says that **God loves us** and created us to have a relationship with Him. His love is strong and intense. But He does ask us to live a life pleasing to Him. The sad thing is we have all sinned just like Adam and Eve in the garden. **Our sins** separate us from God. Sin breaks the relationship we have with Him, and sin brings death upon our lives. We die physically and our souls will also die in hell. Some people believe their **sins can be removed** by being "good enough" and that because of their good deeds God will let them into heaven. However, the Bible says our good works don't get us into heaven. We can never be good enough. But because God loves us, He sent His Son, Jesus, to take on Himself our punishment for our sins. **Jesus paid** for our sins by dying and rising from the dead. He has provided a way for our sins to be completely forgiven. When we stand before God, He doesn't see our sin problem because Jesus has removed our sins. So **everyone who trusts** in Jesus alone can experience eternal life with God in heaven. Trusting in Jesus is when we believe in what He did at the cross and accept Him into our lives. To have Jesus in our lives means our **lives will change**. Jesus will send the Holy Spirit in every believer's life, and the Holy Spirit will help us change. We'll do less and less of the "bad" things and more and more of the things that please God.

When you are finished sharing, ask them what they think. If you sense they are receptive of what you are saying, you could ask them if they would like a relationship with Jesus today. If they say yes, you could ask them to say a prayer with you. They could repeat it after you.

Here's a prayer you could pray. It's not so much the prayer but the heart behind the prayer that matters. *"Dear Lord, thank You that You love me! I'm sorry that my sins have hurt our relationship. Thank You for sending Your Son, Jesus, to die in my place—to take my punishment on Himself. I believe in what Jesus did for me, and I put my faith and trust in Him. I accept the Holy Spirit into my life and ask that He help me live the life now that You want me to live. Thank You that I can go to heaven, and help me share this new faith so others can also come to You. In Jesus' name, I pray, amen."*

As a new believer, let them know of the three ways they can grow in their faith:

1. **Communicate with God through prayer and by reading the Word of God.** If they don't have a Bible, get them one or ask your church if they could provide one for them. Encourage them to start in Matthew so they can read about and see the life of Jesus.

2. **Hang out with other Christians**. The Bible says we become like those we hang out with. So we need to surround ourselves with other Christians so we are less likely to fall away from our commitment.

3. **Get involved in church.** Church is a great way to hang out with other believers (whether with the adults or with the youth ministry) and to learn new truths about God from the teachers and pastors. What a great way to learn about God and grow in our faith and understanding.

Perhaps this seemed like a lot and like a huge endeavor. Let's be an Ezra and study, study, study! God's hand will be on you. He won't leave you or forsake you. Trust that His Holy Spirit will help you.

Let's close with a prayer. *"Dear Lord, help me to know what to say. Prepare a person tomorrow that I could share with. God, I'm not perfect, but I know Your Spirit will work through my imperfections so as to touch a heart tomorrow. Thank You. In Jesus' name, amen!"*

Testimony or Comments:

_____

_____

_____

_____

_____

_____

_____

_____

_____

Day 39

Thursday

I Shared Jesus

TODAY IS THE DAY! Are you nervous? Sure you are, and so am I. I said you never get over being nervous. You do become more comfortable and more confident as you let God use you more. Today I would like you to read **John 14:6, Acts 4:12 and 1 John 5:1, 11–13**. These verses are crucial in sharing your faith because they destroy the thought that anyone can get into heaven as long as they are good enough. These verses make it clear that Jesus is the only way to heaven. If we really believe it, then we need to share it. Unfortunately, many, many Christians don't believe it and as a result they don't share Jesus with lost souls, including their family and friends.

I once heard someone share this information at a conference, but I do not remember who the speaker was.

- According to the last 2010 census, almost 7 billion people are living in the world today.

- Of the 7 billion, 2.1 billion people profess to be Christians. I'm not saying they are all Christians but that they are professing to be Christians. For the sake of argument let's assume they are all Christians.

- That means that 4.9 billion people on the earth today

claim *not* to be Christians. That's 70 percent of the earth's population.

- Approximately 155,000 people die every day across the world.

- That means that 108,500 people (70 percent of those who die every day) enter through hell's gate every day.

- That's 4,520 people every hour.

- That's about 75 people every minute.

- That is easily one person every second. So we could easily say that every second someone dies and spends eternity in the lake of fire called hell. **Do you capture any sense of URGENCY?**

The Bible speaks of hell as a true and real place. Here are some Scripture verses to read:

- *[God's judgment] will happen when the Lord Jesus is revealed from heaven in blazing fire with his powerful angels. He will punish those who do not know God and do not obey the gospel of our Lord Jesus. They will be punished with everlasting destruction and shut out from the presence of the Lord and from the majesty of his power.* (**2 Thessalonians 1:7b–9**)

- *The lake of fire is the second death.* (**Revelation 20:14**)

- *If anyone's name was not found written in the book of life, he was thrown into the lake of fire.* (**Revelation 20:15**)

- *Throw them into the fiery furnace, where there will be weeping and gnashing of teeth.* (**Matthew 13:50**)

- *Where "their worm does not die, and the fire is not quenched."* (**Mark 9:48**)

- *[The beast] will be tormented with burning sulfur.* (**Revelation 14:10**)

- *The smoke of their torment rises for ever and ever. There is no rest day or night for those who worship the beast.* (**Revelation 14:11**)

Read **Ezekiel 3:18–19**. We pass by people every day who don't know Christ as their Lord and Savior. Let God use us to share His love by how we act and what we say. God recognized the need for people's lives to be saved from the penalty of sin, and so He sent His Son, Jesus, to die and take our punishment on Himself. And now He asks us to do our part by sharing the GOSPEL message. Read **Acts 1:8** and **Matthew 28:18–20**

> **Here is your challenge: Pray that God will provide you with an opportunity to start a conversation with someone that leads you to share your faith with them by sharing the GOSPEL message.**

Here are some suggestions in hopes of making it easier.

1. During the 40-day challenge, you have been praying for five people you know who don't know Jesus. You could call one or all of them and see how they are doing. Then you could share how you are doing this 40-day challenge and today is Day 39, which has to do with heaven and hell. Tell them you want to find out what people believe about heaven and hell and ask if they would like to share what they believe. If they say no, ask if they would listen to you share what you believe. If they say no again, then be very kind and respectful of their position. Don't be discouraged, because the fact that someone says no means the Holy Spirit is convicting their heart. They aren't ready to hear the truth verbally, but the Holy Spirit lets them feel the truth in their heart. That's progress. If, however, they are willing to share their belief on heaven and hell,

then listen to all they have to say without interrupting or correcting them. When they are finished, thank them for being open and honest, then ask if you could share what you believe. If they say yes, then now is the opportunity to share the GOSPEL message. No matter how they respond, God will use this. They may have questions, so be honest with the answers. If you don't know the answers, tell them you don't know but would gladly find out for them.

2. You may want to contact someone you have already reached out to during the 40-day challenge because once you connect with someone, they are more receptive to what you have to say about the Lord. So contact them and let them know about today being heaven and hell day.

3. Pray for God to reveal someone who has a specific need that you could reach out to and connect with. You may see a complete stranger or someone you know in need on the road, on the sidewalk, in a store, in a classroom, in the cafeteria, or at work. It could be a problem with something they own, or an emotional problem. When you help them, pray for God to open the door for a conversation to lead into the chance to share the GOSPEL message.

4. Some people take a Bible, or Bible tract, and pray for God to show them someone who could use the Bible. You could ask a person who looks lonely, depressed or in need if they would like a Bible. If they say yes, then take advantage of the opportunity to ask if the person has any needs you could pray for. This often leads into asking if they have a relationship with Jesus, which leads into sharing the GOSPEL message.

5. You could take the Greg Stier approach. Greg Stier, from Dare 2 Share, will often be in a normal conversation with someone but will turn it into a conversation about the love of Jesus. For example, one guy got into a conversa-

tion with Greg about a beautiful, fast car, which led into a conversation about how quickly one would die if it crashed going at a high rate of speed, which led Greg into stating that he knows where he would go, which led into a discussion about heaven and hell, which led into a discussion about Jesus being the way to heaven.

6. There are many ways the Holy Spirit can use us in sharing the GOSPEL message. I don't want to limit Him in any way. Be open for His leading, and be ready to act upon the open door.

Like I said yesterday, when you are finished sharing, ask them what they think. If you sense they are receptive of what you are saying, you could ask them if they would like a relationship with Jesus today. If they say yes, you could ask them to say a prayer with you. They could repeat it after you.

Here's a prayer you could pray. It's not so much the prayer but the heart behind the prayer that matters. *"Dear Lord, thank You that You love me! I'm sorry that my sins have hurt our relationship. Thank You for sending Your Son, Jesus, to die in my place—to take my punishment on Himself. I believe in what Jesus did for me, and I put my faith and trust in Him. I accept the Holy Spirit into my life and ask that He help me live the life now that You want me to live. Thank You that I can go to heaven, and help me share this new faith so others can also come to You. In Jesus' name, I pray, amen."*

As a new believer, let them know of the three ways they can grow in their faith:

1. **Communicate with God through prayer and by reading the Word of God.** If they don't have a Bible, get them one or ask your church if they could provide one for them. Encourage them to start in Matthew so they can read about and see the life of Jesus.

2. **Hang out with other Christians.** The Bible says we become like those we hang out with. So we need to surround ourselves with other Christians so we are less likely to fall away from our commitment.

3. **Get involved in church.** Church is a great way to hang out with other believers (whether with the adults or with the youth ministry) and to learn from teachers about the truth of God's Word. What a great way to learn about God and grow in our faith and understanding.

Let's close with a prayer. *"Dear Lord, reveal to me who You would want me to share with today. Give me the words to say. Speak through me. Help me to not be discouraged if they are not receptive, because I know You are at work in their lives. Thank You. In Jesus' name, amen!"*

Testimony or Comments:

_____

_____

_____

_____

_____

_____

_____

_____

_____

Day 40

Now I Remember

WHEN I WAS IN SECOND GRADE, I had an experience that I'll never forget! My mom had knitted some new mittens for us kids, and we wore them to school on those cold days. They were nice mittens and served their purpose very well. She put a lot of work into them. On one particular day, our second grade classroom went outside for recess up on the hill in Union City. I have fond memories of that playground. It had monkey bars, a teeter-totter, swing sets, one of those . . .I forgot what they call them . . . like a merry-go-round. It was a round "thing" that you spin in a circle and jump on—then you hang on for your dear life. There was also a huge rock on the edge of the playground property. We loved to climb the rock. I remember a certain formation in the rock that I often put my hand on in order to help me get on top of the rock. I remember the playground having a lot of space for running and chasing.

During recess on this particular day, my hands got warm from all the "hard" playing, and I took my mittens off and put them on the playground bench. When it came time for our class to line up and go in, I was not paying attention. I finally realized that my teacher had already left, and I darted off that playground so fast that I forgot all about my mittens. As I ran down

171

the hill toward the school, my neighbor was yelling my name. I thought he was just saying good-bye, so I waved at him with my hand while keeping my eyes focused forward so I could catch up with the rest of my classmates. Little did I know that my neighbor had my mittens and was trying to get my attention to return them to me. Had I just looked back, I could have saved myself some major aggravation.

When I was on the bus going home that afternoon, my neighbor said he was yelling to me that day because I forgot my mittens. MY MITTENS! I asked where they were now, and he said that his teacher told him to keep them on the playground bench. Oh great! Anyway, after returning home, my mom asked where my mittens were, and I told her I left them at school. She told me to *not* leave them at school but to bring them home every day. Needless to say, the next day the mittens were nowhere to be found. So for the next three days, I told my mom I forgot my mittens. Finally, my mom tied a string on one of my fingers as a reminder to *not forget* my mittens. Even then I didn't have the heart to tell the truth, so I wore the string all day, including on the bus. When I got home that afternoon, she asked where my mittens were, and I finally told her the truth. I won't tell you the rest of the story, but I will say she wasn't very happy!

The point I want to emphasize is there were three events:

- Mom made beautiful mittens.
- I lost the mittens.
- Mom put a string on my finger.

The string was to remind me to remember to bring my mittens home. What the string did instead was remind me that I lost the beautiful mittens, and I feared for "my life" (okay, not really for "my life," but I was afraid of getting in trouble).

In the Old Testament, when something happened that God wanted His people to always remember, He would have them do certain things which acted as reminders of His great works.

Read **Exodus 13:1–10.** God promised the Israelites, who were slaves in Egypt, that He would deliver them from slavery. He would take them out of Egypt and on a journey which would eventually end across the Jordan River and in the Promised Land. The new land He would take them to would be flowing with an abundance of food and drink. This was God's promise! As a reminder of God delivering them with His mighty hand, He told His people to do something every year. The same time every year, they were to perform a ceremony that required them to eat unleavened bread (bread without yeast) for seven days. And on the seventh day, they were to have a festival. This seven-day ceremony served two purposes:

1. It was to be a reminder of how God delivered them out of Egypt with His mighty hand. They were also to tell their children this when they asked, "Why are we doing this?"

2. It was also to act as a reminder to stay obedient to God's laws.

During their journey from Egypt to the Promised Land, the Israelites encountered several obstacles. And through each obstacle, God delivered them. They encountered the Red Sea, the lack of food and water, foreign people who hated them, accusations, and so on. It took over 40 years before they actually crossed the Jordan River and walked into the Promised Land.

Now read **Joshua 4:1–9.** Crossing the Jordan River was no easy task. It was at flood stage, meaning it would be 10–12 feet deep with a powerful current. But as the Israelites stepped into the water, by faith and obedience, God parted the water like He did the Red Sea, and they crossed over on dry land.

As a reminder of this great act, God commanded the people to take 12 stones and place them on the Promised Land as a memorial of His great work. It was to remind them always of when God cut off the water so they could cross over on dry land. And as their children grew up and asked why the rocks were there, it served as an opportunity to share with them of the great thing God did in that place.

Your challenge for Day 40 is to not eat bread with yeast and to put down some stones. Okay, I'm kidding. But I want you to do something as a reminder of what God did in and through your life over these last 39 days.

Think of the 39 challenges you have been given, and write down some of the things you did and experienced as a reminder of God's mighty hand. This will be important because a day will come when you will be discouraged and will begin to question God's existence. What you write down today will be a reminder of God's mighty hand and a reminder to stay faithful and obedient to His call on your life. After you write them down, keep your list in a place where you will readily see it. I would love to hear of your testimonies.

Thanks so very much for doing these challenges. I know it was not always easy, but now I pray that your time with God has become so important and such a part of your life that you will continue having daily Bible and prayer time with the Lord. Keep reading, keep praying, keep serving others, keep sharing your faith, keep going to church and keep hanging out with other Christians.

Write down a few testimonies of what God did over the last 39 devotionals:

Testimony or Comments:

_____

_____

_____

_____

_____

_____

_____

_____

_____

_____

_____

_____

After you write down some of your testimonies, I would love to have you e-mail me what God has done so I can share them with others for the glory of God. My e-mail is Blair@BlairBlakeslee.com, or Facebook me under **Blair Blakeslee.**

Challenge of ALL Challenges

Day 41

Saturday

Living for Jesus Every Day

CONGRATULATIONS! You did it! You completed the 40-day devotional challenge. How do you feel? Do you feel a sense of accomplishment? Do you feel you have grown closer to the Lord? Was it hard or easy? I'm sure you have a variety of feelings going through your heart and mind. Whatever those feelings are, please feel good about yourself. I praise the Lord for your willingness to invest your life and time with Him by putting your faith into practice. Now comes the CHALLENGE OF ALL CHALLENGES!

In **John 19**, starting with verse 28, we read about the death of Jesus on the cross. At one moment He cried out, "It is finished!" Jesus did *not* mean He was defeated or that He was dead forever or that He was never coming back. Instead Jesus was saying that He had now completed the work that He came to earth to do out of obedience to His Father. Jesus just finished shedding His blood and dying for our sins. Forgiveness is no longer found in the sacrifice of animals, for Jesus made the ultimate sacrifice, once and for all, that is necessary for our salvation (**Hebrews 9:22, 26; 1 Peter 3:18**).

Jesus finished what was necessary for a new beginning! The new beginning started when He rose from the dead, and now He is at work building His new kingdom (or new body of believers). We are His instruments that He wants to use to accomplish this work. So though we are now finished with the 40-day devotional challenge, my prayer is that we would see a new beginning. My hope is that our hearts have become more in love with Jesus and that we have a new desire to live out our faith for Him.

I pray we no longer need a book that says, "Meet with God in your devotions at 6:00 tomorrow morning." I hope by now we are looking forward to spending time alone with God. It would be great if you keep meeting with Him during the times you established and keep growing in your faith. I pray that we no longer need a book that says, "Pick up your room today as a way of honoring your parents," or "Buy flowers for your wife," or "Fix a nice meal for your husband," or "Apologize to your boss or teacher for the disrespect you showed them." I hope that serving Jesus by serving others has become so much a part of our lives that we automatically will look for ways to love our parents, our enemies, our neighbors, our authority figures, our church friends, and so on.

I pray our hearts have become so much more sensitive to the Holy Spirit and His leading that we will be "doing" more with our faith. As a result, more lives will continue to be impacted. I hope that those who saw a change in our lives the last 40 days will continue to see even more changes. We don't want temporary change but an ongoing, lifelong change. Sure, we will have our good days and our bad days. We will continue to make mistakes, but hopefully we will see less and less of these mistakes because we are seeking God with great passion. As a result of this passion, God will slowly be conforming us into the image of His Son, Jesus.

In closing, I would like to quote two passages. First, in **John 13:34–35** Jesus said these words: *"A new command I give you: Love one another. As I have loved you, so you must love one another. By this all men will know that you are my disciples, if you love one another."* And second, in **Matthew 5:16** Jesus said, *"In the same way, let your light shine before men, that they may see your good deeds and praise your Father in heaven."* What more can be said? If we are living out the love of Jesus and letting His life shine through us, eventually we will see people drawn to the Savior of the world in praise and adoration. That's our goal—to reach lost souls.

Once a year I'll redo a devotional challenge to help me get refocused. Maybe you could do the same. God bless you as you live out your faith.

Made in the USA
Charleston, SC
21 July 2012